MW01626043

climb
clamber
scale

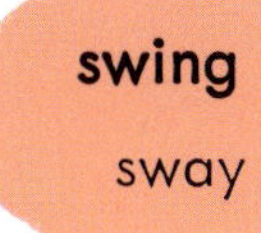

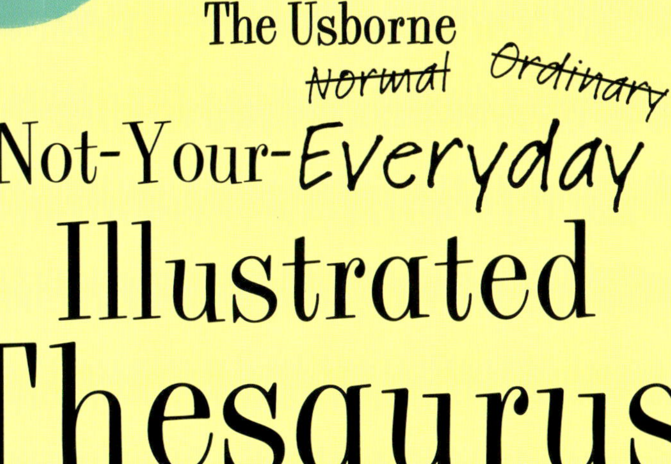

The Usborne ~~Normal~~ ~~Ordinary~~ Not-Your-Everyday Illustrated Thesaurus

hairy
shaggy
furry

caw

James Maclaine

Designed by Emily Barden
Additional designs by Lucy Wain

Edited by Fiona Watt

Illustrated by Susanna Rumiz,
Ilias Sounas, Peter Donnelly, Mark Ruffle,
and The Boy Fitz Hammond

American editor: Carrie Armstrong

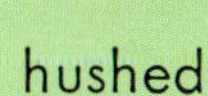

silent
quiet

About this book

What is a thesaurus?

A thesaurus gives you lists of different words that have the same or a similar meaning.

How can I find a word?

This thesaurus divides the lists of words into topics. Search through the contents on page 4 to find the topic you want to know about.

The lists of words look like this:

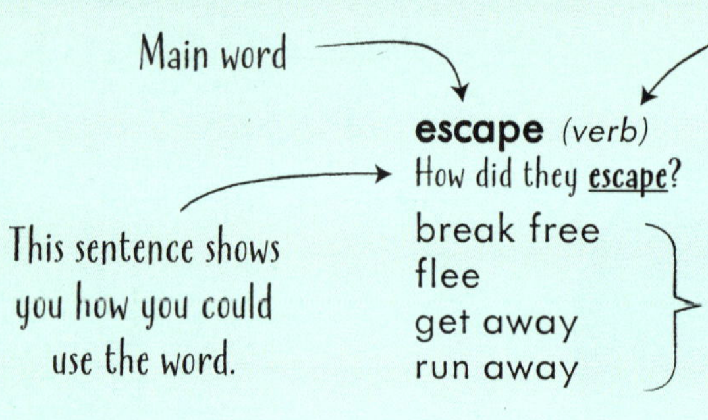

This shows you what type of word it is – whether it is a noun, adjective, verb, adverb or preposition. See opposite to find out what these are.

Instead of escape, you could use any of the words listed below it.

Word finder

You can also look up a particular word in the word finder on pages 108-128, which is in alphabetical order. For example:

big *(adjective)*, 5
bike *(noun)*, 59
bit *(noun)*
see **piece**, 63
bite *(verb)*
see **eat**, 68
bitter *(adjective)*, 70
see **cold**, 33

Look on page 5 to find different words that mean *big*.

To find different words for *bite*, turn to page 68 and look under the main word **eat**.

Some words, such as *bitter*, have more than one meaning. There are lists of words for its different meanings under **bitter** (taste) on page 70, and under **cold** (temperature) on page 33.

Types of words

A **noun** can be a thing, a place, a person or an idea you can think about.

An **adjective** describes a noun.

A **verb** is an action word.

An **adverb** tells you more about a verb or how, when or where something happens.

A **preposition** is a word that connects other words in a sentence to nouns.

noun

The silly clown balanced skillfully on his unicycle.

adjective — verb — adverb — preposition

What else can I find in this book?

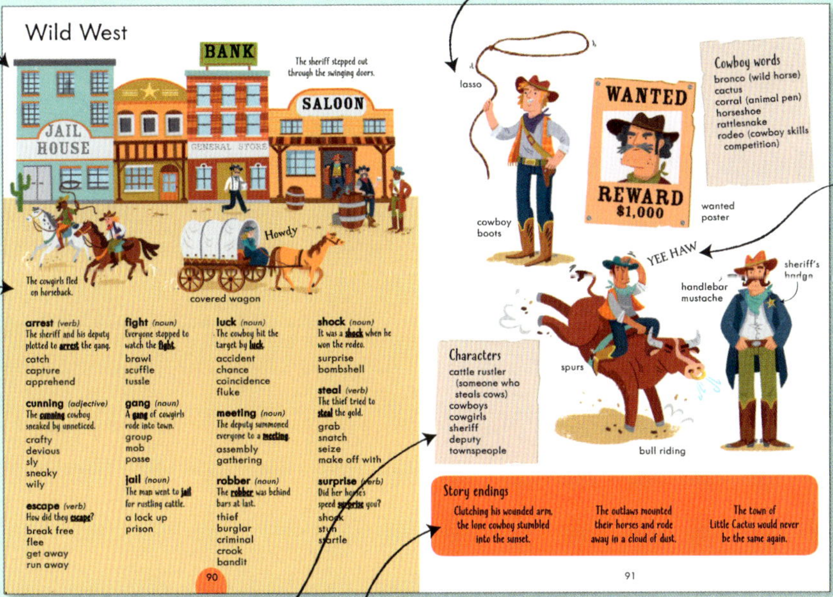

Scenes to write about

More words to use

Sound words

Sentences to inspire your writing

Ideas for characters or names for them

Ways to start or end stories

Wild West

BANK

The sheriff stepped out through the swinging doors.

JAIL HOUSE

GENERAL STORE

SALOON

Howdy

The cowgirls fled on horseback.

covered wagon

arrest *(verb)*
The sheriff and his deputy plotted to **arrest** the gang.
catch
capture
apprehend

cunning *(adjective)*
The **cunning** cowboy sneaked by unnoticed.
crafty
devious
sly
sneaky
wily

escape *(verb)*
How did they **escape**?
break free
flee
get away
run away

fight *(noun)*
Everyone stopped to watch the **fight**.
brawl
scuffle
tussle

gang *(noun)*
A **gang** of cowgirls rode into town.
group
mob
posse

jail *(noun)*
The man went to **jail** for rustling cattle.
a lock up
prison

luck *(noun)*
The cowboy hit the target by **luck**.
accident
chance
coincidence
fluke

meeting *(noun)*
The deputy summoned everyone to a **meeting**.
assembly
gathering

robber *(noun)*
The **robber** was behind bars at last.
thief
burglar
criminal
crook
bandit

shock *(noun)*
It was a **shock** when he won the rodeo.
surprise
bombshell

steal *(verb)*
The thief tried to **steal** the gold.
grab
snatch
seize
make off with

surprise *(verb)*
Did her horse's speed **surprise** you?
shock
stun
startle

90

lasso

cowboy boots

WANTED
REWARD
$1,000

wanted poster

Cowboy words
bronco (wild horse)
cactus
corral (animal pen)
horseshoe
rattlesnake
rodeo (cowboy skills competition)

YEE HAW

sheriff's badge

handlebar mustache

spurs

bull riding

Characters
cattle rustler (someone who steals cows)
cowboys
cowgirls
sheriff
deputy
townspeople

Story endings

Clutching his wounded arm, the lone cowboy stumbled into the sunset.

The outlaws mounted their horses and rode away in a cloud of dust.

The town of Little Cactus would never be the same again.

91

There are lots of tips to improve your writing and games to play, on pages 104 – 107.

Contents

Size words

tall *(adjective)*
big
gangling
lanky
lofty
soaring
towering

long *(adjective)*
elongated
extended
lengthy
stretched

small *(adjective)*
little
tiny
mini
dainty
miniature
minute
petite
puny
teeny
compact
itty-bitty

thin *(adjective)*
narrow
slim
lean
skinny
slight
slender

big *(adjective)*
The orange-horned monster is so **big**.
huge
large
gigantic
enormous
hulking
immense
bulky
mammoth
massive
overgrown
vast

fat *(adjective)*
chubby
chunky
flabby
hefty
large
plump
pudgy
portly
stocky
stout

short *(adjective)*
My legs are **short**.
squat
stubby
stumpy
squashed

How big?

rather *(adverb)*
The green monster is **rather** big.
a bit
a little
fairly
quite
somewhat

very *(adverb)*
The blue monster is **very** big.
ever so
exceedingly
extremely
really
truly

How many?

few *(adjective)*
Few monsters have horns.
a handful of
hardly any
not many
one or two

many *(adjective)*
Many monsters have tails.
a lot of
countless
lots of
numerous

Colors

Colors can be adjectives or nouns.

red	crimson	cherry	tomato	scarlet	ruby
maroon	pink	magenta	cerise	fuchsia	rose
salmon	coral	orange	amber	apricot	peach
ginger	yellow	lemon	butter	mustard	saffron
gold	ocher	buff	green	lime	acid green
grass green	bottle green	olive	khaki	emerald	jade
blue	turquoise	royal blue	azure	powder blue	sky blue
cobalt	navy	sapphire	purple	indigo	grape

color *(noun)*
hue
shade

Describing colors

bright *(adjective)*
That's a **bright** shade of green.
bold
fluorescent
glaring
loud
lurid
rich
vibrant
vivid

dull *(adjective)*
The colors in the photo are rather **dull**.
dingy
drab
dreary
faded
faint
light
pale
wan

Colors can also be...
clashing
eye-catching
garish
gaudy
muddy

Shapes

Flat (2-D) shapes

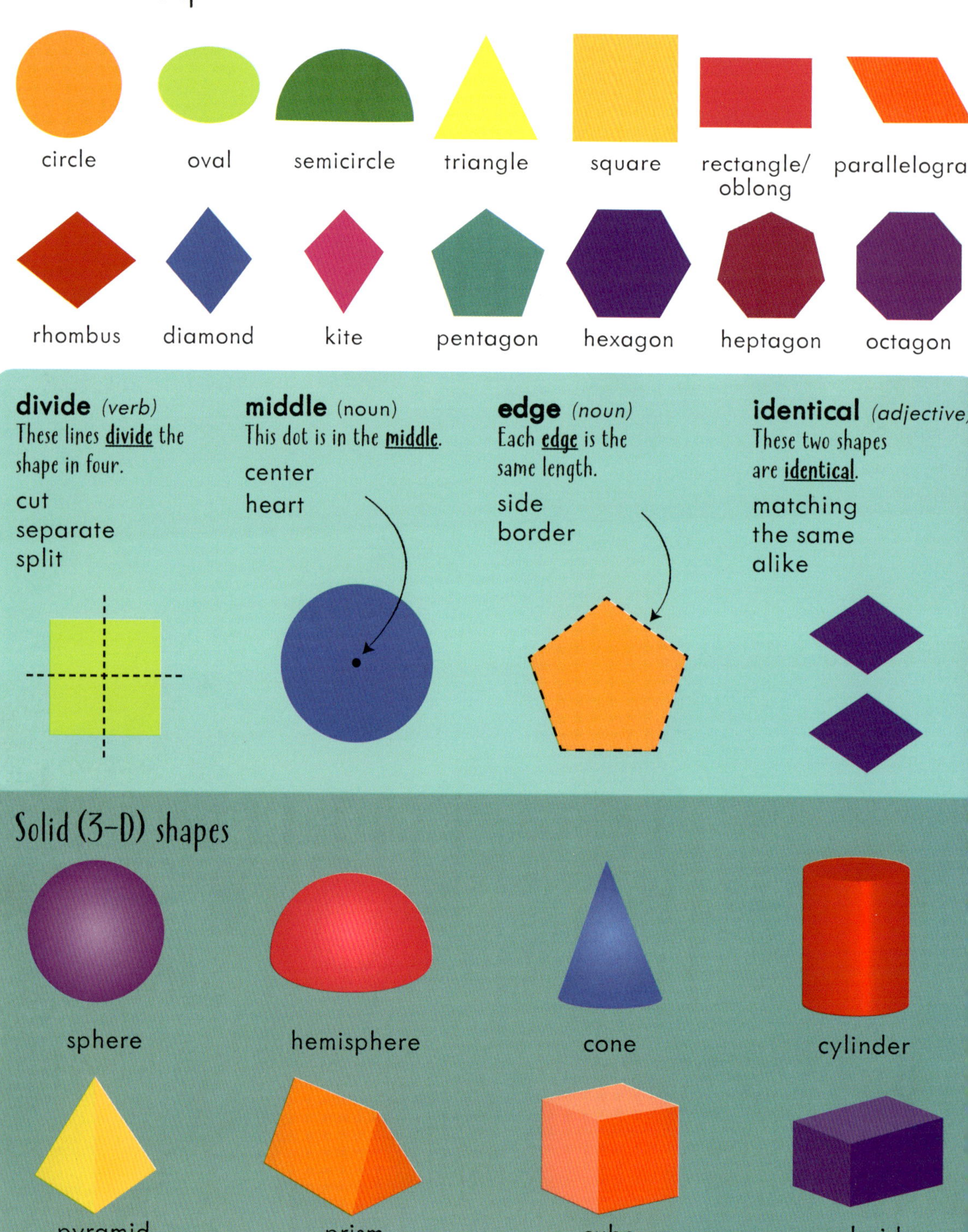

Patterns

complicated
(adjective)
complex
elaborate
intricate
ornate
plain
(adjective)
simple
basic
curly
(adjective)
whirly
swirly
spotted
(adjective)
dotted
flecked
mottled
specked
speckled
checkered
(adjective)
checked
harlequin
patchwork
slurp
striped
(adjective)
banded
lined
even *(adjective)*
All of our patterns are even.
balanced
uniform
regular
zigzag
(adjective)
jagged
wavy

Materials and tools

Describing how materials feel and look

bumpy *(adjective)*
knobbed
lumpy
ridged
uneven

clear *(adjective)*
see-through
transparent

cloudy *(adjective)*
murky
opaque

delicate *(adjective)*
breakable
brittle
flimsy
fragile

dry *(adjective)*
crisp
crispy
dried out
parched

fluffy *(adjective)*
furry
fleecy
downy
shaggy
woolly

hard *(adjective)*
firm
rigid
stiff

heavy *(adjective)*
bulky
hefty
massive
dense

light *(adjective)*
easy-to-carry
lightweight

rough *(adjective)*
coarse
craggy
gnarled
leathery
uneven

sharp *(adjective)*
spiky
jagged
pointed
scratchy
bristly
spiny

smooth *(adjective)*
even
glossy
polished
satiny
sleek

soft *(adjective)*
bouncy
squishy
springy
mushy

solid *(adjective)*
compacted
jam-packed
thick

strong *(adjective)*
durable
hard-wearing
solid
sturdy
tough

wet *(adjective)*
damp
dewy
moist
soggy
soaked

Giving opinions

opinion *(noun)*
What's your **opinion**?
feeling
point of view
view

believe *(verb)*
I used to **believe** this route was best.
think
be of the opinion
be sure
be convinced

better *(adjective)*
This way is **better**.
easier
more effective
preferable

fair *(adjective)*
I think a reward would be a **fair** idea.
appropriate
apt
deserving
fitting
just
proper
suitable

general *(adjective)*
The **general** opinion is that man's a liar.
common
typical
universal

hate *(verb)*
She used to **hate** olives.
dislike
despise
detest
abhor
loathe
have an aversion to

important *(adjective)*
There's an **important** difference between the two.
critical
significant

like *(verb)*
I used to **like** chocolate.
enjoy
love
relish
favor
be partial to

We used to **like** her.
be fond of
be friends with
get along well with

Do you think they'd **like** it?
be interested in
take pleasure in

The children really **like** their granny.
adore
love

likely *(adjective)*
The **likely** result is their team will win.
probable

maybe *(adverb)*
Maybe it will be a draw.
perhaps
possibly

mind *(verb)*
Will you **mind** if I'm late?
be bothered
be upset
care
object

ordinary *(adjective)*
It's a fairly **ordinary** painting.
average
mediocre
unremarkable

possible *(adjective)*
Do you think it's **possible** we will lose?
conceivable
feasible

right *(adjective)*
She gave a **right** answer to the question.
correct
true
valid

seem *(verb)*
How does it **seem** to you?
appear
look

special *(adjective)*
There's something **special** about this movie.
exceptional
first-class
outstanding
unique
unusual

suggest *(verb)*
I **suggest** we go back before it's dark.
advise
propose
recommend
urge

unfair *(adjective)*
It's **unfair** that they can't come too.
unjust
unreasonable

wrong *(adjective)*
The boastful boy gave a **wrong** answer.
false
incorrect
untrue

Nice words

nice *(adjective)*

There's a __nice__ view from my palace.

beautiful
breathtaking
glorious
picturesque
spectacular
splendid

He's a __nice__ host.

courteous
gracious
polite

It was __nice__ of you to lend me your guitar.

helpful
kind
likable
generous
pleasant
sweet

The decorator did a __nice__ job.

careful
neat
professional

We had a __nice__ time at the show.

agreeable
enjoyable
fun
good
great
lovely
marvelous
pleasant
terrific
wonderful

That lunch was __nice__.

delicious
delectable
tasty

The weather is __nice__ today.

beautiful
bright
fair
fine
glorious
pretty
mild

What a __nice__ smell!

aromatic
fragrant

She's such a __nice__ person.

amiable
caring
charming
considerate
delightful
friendly
generous
good-natured
helpful
kind
likable
lovely
pleasant
sweet
unselfish
warm-hearted

I look __nice__ in my new suit.

attractive
beautiful
handsome
lovely
pretty
stunning

Good, bad or okay?

yippee

good
(adjective)

The gardener did a **good** job.

admirable
careful
first-rate
satisfactory
sound
thorough

You're a **good** person.

decent
honest
just
upright
virtuous

They gave a **good** reason for being late.

adequate
genuine
proper
reasonable
valid

We thought the book was **good**.

excellent
fantastic
great
marvelous
stellar
super
superb
terrific
wonderful

The weather is **good** today.

bright
fair
fine
glorious
mild
sunny

They told some **good** stories about their trip.

entertaining
exciting
lively
vivid

My little brother is such a **good** boy.

angelic
helpful
polite
sweet
well-behaved

We had such a **good** time.

enjoyable
fun
interesting
pleasant

She's a **good** tennis player.

accomplished
capable
fine
first-class
gifted
talented

That was a **good** thing to do.

charitable
considerate
kind
thoughtful

You're in a **good** mood.

cheerful
cheery
happy
jolly
positive

bravo

bad
(adjective)

A **bad** man ruled the country.

corrupt
cruel
dishonest
evil
sinful
wicked

I've never read such a **bad** book.

abysmal
appalling
atrocious
dire
lousy

This **bad** weather is depressing.

awful
dismal
dreary
foul
nasty

There was a **bad** accident.

catastrophic
disastrous
dreadful
horrific
serious
terrible

My little sister is such a **bad** girl.

badly-behaved
disobedient
impertinent
mischievous
naughty
rude

The thief felt **bad** about his crimes.

ashamed
guilty
terrible
uneasy
upset

He did a **bad** job.

abysmal
dreadful
inadequate
inferior
poor
unsatisfactory

That's a **bad** habit.

dangerous
harmful
risky
unflattering

Why are you in a **bad** mood?

irritable
lousy
sulky

A **bad** smell came from the disposal.

disgusting
foul
horrible
repulsive
revolting
unpleasant
vile

The old apples are **bad**.

moldy
rancid
rotten
spoiled

okay
(adjective)

I suppose the soup is **okay**.

acceptable
all right
average
O.K.
reasonable
so so
tolerable

What are you like?

character *(noun)*
My oldest friend has a unique **character**.
nature
personality

boring *(adjective)*
dreary
dull
tedious

brave *(adjective)*
courageous
fearless
intrepid
plucky
daring

childish *(adjective)*
babyish
immature
juvenile
young

clever *(adjective)*
bright
brainy
intelligent
sharp
smart
wise

clumsy *(adjective)*
awkward
bungling
uncoordinated

crazy *(adjective)*
insane
mad
wild

curious *(adjective)*
interested
inquisitive

funny *(adjective)*
amusing
comical
hilarious
humorous
witty

generous *(adjective)*
charitable
kind
magnanimous

grumpy *(adjective)*
bad-tempered
crabby
cantankerous
prickly
surly

honest *(adjective)*
honorable
moral
scrupulous
trustworthy
truthful
virtuous

kind *(adjective)*
caring
considerate
sweet
warm-hearted

lively *(adjective)*
bubbly
energetic
exuberant
spirited

lovely *(adjective)*
amiable
charming
delightful
enchanting
engaging

naughty *(adjective)*
disobedient
mischievous
unruly
willful

nosy *(adjective)*
meddlesome
prying

picky *(adjective)*
choosy
fussy
finicky
particular

polite *(adjective)*
considerate
courteous
respectful
well-mannered

proud *(adjective)*
arrogant
conceited
haughty
snobbish
snooty
vain

sensible *(adjective)*
level-headed
practical
thoughtful

serious *(adjective)*
dour
earnest
stern

shy *(adjective)*
bashful
coy
reserved
timid
wary

silly *(adjective)*
featherbrained
foolish
goofy

stupid *(adjective)*
brainless
dim
idiotic
senseless

How do you feel?

feeling *(noun)*
A strange feeling came over me.
emotion
sensation

angry *(adjective)*
enraged
fuming
furious
irate
livid
mad

annoyed *(adjective)*
cross
grumpy
irked
irritated
vexed

bored *(adjective)*
fed up
restless

cold *(adjective)*
chilly
cool
frozen

confused *(adjective)*
baffled
bamboozled
bewildered
disoriented
fazed
mixed-up
perplexed
puzzled

dizzy *(adjective)*
faint
giddy
weak
wobbly

excited *(adjective)*
eager
ecstatic
enthusiastic
frenzied
keen
thrilled

full *(adjective)*
satisfied
stuffed
well-fed

happy *(adjective)*
cheerful
chirpy
delighted
glad
jolly
joyful
perky
pleased

hot *(adjective)*
feverish
flushed

hungry *(adjective)*
famished
ravenous
starving

sad *(adjective)*
depressed
down
forlorn
gloomy
glum
heartbroken
low
miserable

scared *(adjective)*
afraid
alarmed
disturbed
frightened
terrified

sick *(adjective)*
ailing
ill
peaky
unwell

sorry *(adjective)*
ashamed
guilty

surprised *(adjective)*
amazed
astonished
astounded
shocked
startled
stunned
thunderstruck

tired *(adjective)*
drowsy
exhausted
sleepy
weary
worn out

upset *(adjective)*
angry
hurt
shaken
worried

well *(adjective)*
fine
fit
healthy
in good shape

worried *(adjective)*
anxious
frantic
fretful
nervous
on edge
tense

People

baby *(noun)*
newborn
little one
infant

child *(noun)*
boy
girl
kid
toddler

teenager *(noun)*
teen
youth
youngster
adolescent

adult *(noun)*
grown-up

How people look

attractive *(adjective)*
You're very **attractive**.
beautiful
good-looking
handsome
pretty

old *(adjective)*
His wrinkles made him look **old**.
aged
elderly

ugly *(adjective)*
You're not **ugly**.
ordinary-looking
plain
unattractive

young *(adjective)*
She looks **young** for her age.
fresh-faced
youthful

Writing about faces

face *(noun)*
I'd describe his **face** as striking.
appearance
features
visage

Faces can be...
angular
babyish
chubby
flushed
freckled
oval
rosy
strong-jawed
stubbly
tanned
wrinkled

Features:
beard
cheek
chin
dimple
eye
eyebrow
forehead
freckle
mole
mustache
nose
pimple
scar
wrinkle

Making faces

scowl *(verb)*
Don't **scowl**!
frown
glower
glare

smile *(verb)*
Your aunt will **smile** when she sees you.
beam
grin

Parts of the body

body *(noun)*
The girl had a small <u>**body**</u>.
figure

Describing hair

hair *(noun)*
That woman has pretty <u>**hair**</u>.
locks

Hair colors:
auburn
black
blonde
chestnut
dark
fair
gray
brown
red
strawberry blonde

Hair can be...
braided
bushy
curly
dyed
fine
flat
frizzy
greasy
lank
shaved
spiky
tousled
wavy

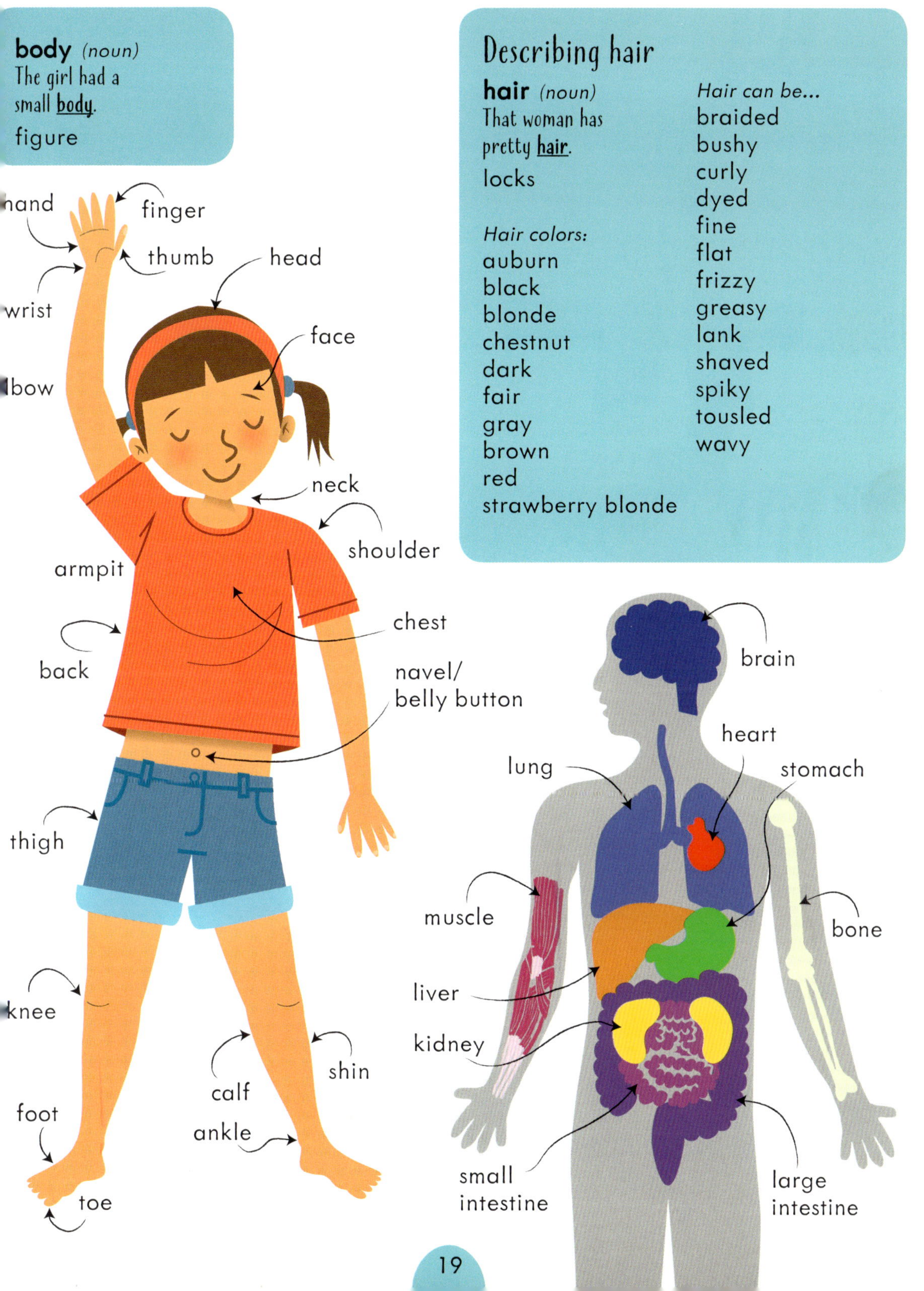

Flowers, plants and trees

flower *(noun)*
There was just one <u>flower</u> on the bush.
bloom

Some types of flowers:

anemone
bluebell
carnation
chrysanthemum
cornflower
cowslip
crocus
daffodil
dahlia
daisy
forget-me-not
foxglove
freesia
geranium
hollyhock
hyacinth
iris
lavender
lily
marigold
orchid
poppy
rose
sunflower
sweet pea
tulip
violet
zinnia

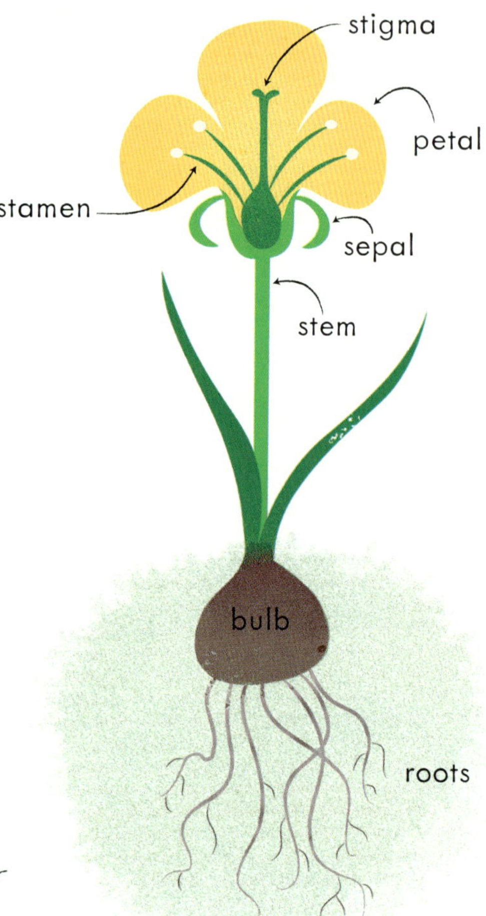

A bumblebee made a gentle humming sound as it flitted from flower to flower.

dandelion

The gentle breeze dispersed the seeds far and wide.

plant *(noun)*
Types of plants:

bulb
bush
cactus
climber
fern
grass
moss
shrub
succulent
vine
weed
wildflower

Some plants, called annuals, live for one year only. A perennial plant lives year after year.

tree *(noun)*

Types of trees:

ash
aspen
beech
birch
bonsai
cedar
cherry
cypress
dogwood
elm
eucalyptus
fir
gingko
hazel
horse chestnut
juniper
laburnum
magnolia
maple
oak
olive
pine
poplar
rowan
spruce
sweetgum
sycamore
willow
yew

Animal words

animal *(noun)*
What type of <u>animal</u> is it?
creature
beast

Places, or habitats, where animals live:
desert
grassland
mangrove
meadow
mountains
pond
rainforest
swamp
wetland
wood

Types of animals

mammals
aardvark
bat
chimpanzee
deer
hippopotamus
kangaroo
lion
panda
seal
tiger
walrus

birds
blackbird
cockatoo
dove
eagle
flamingo
kingfisher
magpie
ostrich

amphibians
frog
newt
salamander
toad

invertebrates
beetle
dragonfly
earthworm
fly
lobster
scorpion
snail
spider
squid
starfish

reptiles
alligator
crocodile
lizard
python
tortoise
turtle

fish
angelfish
carp
goldfish
piranha
sea horse
shark
stickleback

A wetland habitat

For some animals, there are different names for the females, males and babies.

animal	female	male	baby
pig	sow	boar	piglet
goat	nanny-goat	billy-goat	kid
deer	doe	stag	fawn
rabbit	doe	buck	kit
elephant	cow	bull	calf
chicken	hen	rooster	chick
dog	bitch	dog	puppy
cat	cat	tomcat	kitten
duck	duck	drake	duckling
fox	vixen	fox	cub
goose	goose	gander	gosling
kangaroo	doe	buck	joey
lion	lioness	lion	cub
horse	mare	stallion	foal
sheep	ewe	ram	lamb

Groups of animals

a swarm of insects
a herd of deer
a school of fish
a brood of chicks
a litter of puppies

a flock of birds
a pack of wolves
a pod of dolphins
a pride of lions
a flock of sheep

a gaggle of geese
an army of frogs
a streak of tigers
a troop of monkeys
a colony of bats

Describing animals

furry *(adjective)*
Orangutans have __furry__ coats.
fluffy
fuzzy
hairy
woolly

smooth *(adjective)*
The __smooth__-skinned gecko scuttled up the wall.
silky
velvety

Animals can be...
agile
feathery
lop-eared
poisonous
scaly
shy
sly
speckled
tame
tufted
venomous
vicious
warty
wild

Animals may have...
antlers
beaks
curved claws
fangs
forked tongues
glossy feathers
hooves
horns
paws
stripes
tails
trunks
whiskers

Words for animals that describe what they eat:
- herbivores eat plants and fruit.
- carnivores eat meat.
- omnivores eat everything.

Cats, dogs and other pets

Cat words

cat *(noun)*
kitty
kitty-cat

Types of cats:
Burmese
long-haired cat
Manx cat
short-haired cat
Siamese
tabby
tortoiseshell

meow *(verb)*
Did you hear the cats <u>meow</u>?

cry
mew

canary

parakeet

Dog words

dog *(noun)*
hound
mutt
pooch

Types of dogs:
beagle
bloodhound
boxer
corgi
dachshund
dalmatian
foxhound
golden retriever
greyhound
husky
labrador
mixed-breed
poodle
pug
spaniel
terrier
whippet

bark *(verb)*
My dogs <u>bark</u> when the doorbell rings.

woof
growl
yelp
yowl

Other pet words

Other types of pets:
canary
gerbil
goldfish
guinea pig
hamster
mouse
parakeet
parrot
pony
rabbit
rat
snake

Pets can...
creep
curl up
frisk
frolic
jump
leap
nuzzle
scamper
scratch
slink
sprawl

Pets can live in a...
cage
hutch
kennel
stable
tank

tame *(adjective)*
Pets are <u>tame</u> animals.

gentle
obedient
well-behaved

Pets can also be...
affectionate
alert
curious
friendly
lazy
loyal
mischievous
playful
sleepy
timid

Some pets' fur can be...
fluffy
glossy
mangy
matted
rough
shaggy
shiny
silky
smooth
soft
wiry

Animals sometimes sit on their rear haunches.

Insect words

insect *(noun)*
The <u>insect</u> skittered out of sight.

bug
creepy crawly

Insects can...
bite
buzz
crawl
dart
flit
flutter
fly
hide
hover
scurry
scuttle
sting

become *(verb)*
Inside its chrysalis a caterpillar will <u>become</u> a butterfly.

change into
develop into
grow into
turn into

Bird sounds

squawk *(verb)*
Birds squawk.

chatter
cheep
chirp
chirrup
cluck
crow
hoot
pipe
screech
sing
trill
twitter
warble
whistle

Noisy words

noise *(noun)*
The chattering crowds made such a **noise**.

clamor
din
hullabaloo
racket
row
rumpus
sound
tumult

SCREECH
DING DONG
BOOM
POP
SQUEAK
BING
CLOMP
CLATTER
WHAM
CLANG
THWACK
THUD

Sounds

alarm *(noun)*
An **alarm** whined in the street below.

bell
siren

bang *(noun)*
The firework went off with a loud **bang**.

boom
explosion
pop

Describing sounds

deep *(adjective)*
The ogre made a **deep** groan.

low
booming
low-pitched

high *(adjective)*
He blew a **high** note on his whistle.

high-pitched
piercing
sharp
shrill

loud *(adjective)*
A **loud** bang resounded.

noisy
booming
ear-splitting
deafening

noisy *(adjective)*
The children were rather **noisy**.

boisterous
chatty
raucous
rowdy
talkative

quiet *(adjective)*
They spoke in **quiet** voices so as not to wake the dragon.

hushed
muffled
muted
soft

BANG

Noisy things may...

burst *(verb)*
I hate it when balloons **burst**.

explode
go bang
go pop

ring *(verb)*
The bells **ring** through the town.

chime
ding
jingle
peal
ping

roar *(verb)*
Did you hear the thunder **roar**?

boom
rumble

splash *(verb)*
Can you hear the stream **splash**?

babble
bubble
gurgle

Noisy things may also...

blare
blast
buzz
click
crunch
fizz
sizzle
twang

crash

Actions

bend *(verb)*
I must bend down and tie my shoelaces.

crouch
lean
squat
stoop

break *(verb)*
It's impossible to break this bowl.

chip
crack
damage
destroy
ruin
shatter
smash
wreck

bump *(verb)*
Try not to bump your head.

bang
bash
knock

carry *(verb)*
He can't carry that box.

bear
bring
haul
hold
lug
move

climb *(verb)*
There's still time to climb the tower.

go up
clamber up
ascend
scale

crawl *(verb)*
You will have to crawl through that gap.

go on all fours
move on hands and knees

creep *(verb)*
We have to creep past the sleeping dragon.

sneak
slink
inch
tiptoe

cry *(verb)*
Please try not to cry.

weep
snivel
sob
blub

cut *(verb)*
I need someone to cut my hair.

clip
snip
trim

die *(verb)*
They feared their leader might die.

pass away

dive *(verb)*
She began to dive through the air.

plunge
pitch
plummet
nosedive

fall *(verb)*
Be careful or you'll fall.

slip
stumble
trip
tumble

find *(verb)*
What did you find in the shadows?

spot
discover
hit upon
locate
come across
stumble upon

follow *(verb)*
Follow that car!

chase
go after
pursue
shadow
tail

get off *(verb)*
We need to get off at the next stop.

alight
disembark
dismount
get out

get on *(verb)*
The man tried to get on the train.

board
enter
climb aboard

give *(verb)*
Will you give the money to me?

hand over
offer
present
supply

grip *(verb)*
You must grip the bars tightly.

clutch
grasp

hug *(verb)*
The boy had to hug his teddy so he could sleep.

cling to
cuddle
embrace

jump *(verb)*
Don't jump on the bed.

bounce
leap
spring

kill *(verb)*
They plotted to kill the king.

murder
assassinate
slay

lead *(verb)*
Can you lead me to the gallery?
direct
guide

leave *(verb)*
When do you plan to leave?
go
depart
make tracks
set off

look *(verb)*
I won't look!
watch
gaze
observe
peer
gawp

meet *(verb)*
The soldiers meet at noon.
assemble
come together
gather
get together

perform *(verb)*
They perform on stage.
act
appear

pick up *(verb)*
Can you pick up the bread from the bakery?
collect
fetch
get

poke *(verb)*
Did you poke me?
prod
jab
nudge
elbow

pull *(verb)*
They tried to pull the rope.
haul
heave
tug
yank

push *(verb)*
Push the clothes into the bag.
press
shove
squeeze
thrust

put *(verb)*
Can you put it on the table?
lay
leave
place
plonk
set

reach *(verb)*
When will they reach the house?
appear at
arrive at
come to
get to
show up at

run *(verb)*
We have to run.
dash
jog
race
rush
scamper
scurry
sprint

shake *(verb)*
The musicians shake their maracas.
jiggle
rattle

shut *(verb)*
Don't forget to shut the windows.
close
lock
bolt

sit *(verb)*
Let me sit here for a moment.
perch
squat

spray *(verb)*
Can you spray some water on the roses?
splash
squirt

spread *(verb)*
Let's spread the blanket here.
arrange
open out
unroll

squash *(verb)*
You can use your foot to squash it.
crush
crumple
flatten

stand *(verb)*
Please stand when the teacher comes in.
get up
rise

take *(verb)*
When did he take the candy?
get
grab
receive
seize
snatch

touch *(verb)*
Don't touch the material.
feel
finger
handle

twist *(verb)*
Would you help me twist the cable?
wind
coil

wave *(verb)*
Don't wave your finger at me!
shake
twirl
waggle

Get, go, do...

You might use some verbs, such as get, go and do, a lot. Try using some of these alternatives instead.

get (verb)

When will we **get** the answers to the quiz?
- be given
- hear
- receive

It took us a week to **get** home.
- arrive
- reach

Where did you **get** your top?
- buy
- acquire
- come by
- obtain
- purchase

The days **get** shorter as winter looms.
- become
- grow
- turn

We tried to **get** him to come but he refused.
- coax
- convince
- force
- make
- persuade

She went to **get** the drinks.
- bring
- retrieve

Did your dog **get** first prize in the show?
- achieve
- attain
- earn
- gain
- win

go (verb)

The army had to **go** before dusk.
- depart
- leave
- set out

Where did the monster **go** all of a sudden?
- disappear to
- vanish to

Where does this track **go**?
- end up
- lead

Let's **go** this way.
- walk
- hurry
- march
- ramble
- rush
- saunter
- stride
- amble

How does the story **go**?
- develop
- progress
- turn out
- unfold

We have to **go** to New York.
- drive
- fly
- journey
- ride
- speed
- travel
- voyage

The comics **go** on the middle shelf.
- belong

Time can **go** slowly when you're bored.
- go by
- elapse
- pass
- slip by

do *(verb)*

There's so much still to **do**.

accomplish
carry out
finish
undertake

What subject do you **do**?

learn
study

This hotel room will **do**.

be good enough
suffice

Who could **do** the repairs?

arrange
handle
make
manage
organize
prepare
see to
take care of

The boy couldn't **do** the puzzle.

answer
crack
figure out
solve
work out

I hope you'll **do** better next week.

cope
fare
get along
manage
perform

move *(verb)*

They had to **move** carefully past the troll.

advance
journey
proceed

Try not to **move** until I blow the whistle!

change position
fidget

They had to **move** overseas for work.

emigrate
relocate

Let's **move** before nightfall.

get going
get started
go
make a move
set off

Can you **move** your bike to the shed?

bring
carry
shift
take

have to *(verb)*

You **have to** try new things.

must
ought to
need to

let *(verb)*

I will **let** you just this once.

allow
permit

need *(verb)*

The task will **need** more time if it's to be done correctly.

call for
depend on
require

try *(verb)*

I'll **try** to run faster next time.

aim
attempt

want *(verb)*

"What do you **want**?" asked the genie.

crave
desire
dream of
long for
yearn for
wish for

Instead of said

answered *(verb)*
"I don't think so," Dylan answered.
replied
responded

asked *(verb)*
"Can I have some more?" asked Oliver.
begged
demanded
pleaded
questioned

confessed *(verb)*
"It was me!" confessed Asha.
admitted
blurted out
owned up

whispered *(verb)*
"Did you hear that?" whispered Ella.
mumbled
murmured
muttered

thought *(verb)*
"Should I stay?" thought Zac.
brooded
pondered
wondered

shouted *(verb)*
"Don't!" shouted Maisie.
screamed
bellowed
ordered
barked
snapped
yelled

BOO HOO

WAAAAAH

cried *(verb)*
"Help!" cried Archie.
bawled
blubbered
gulped
howled
shrieked
sobbed
squealed
wept
whimpered

ha ha HO HO

laughed *(verb)*
"That's ridiculous," laughed Ali.
chortled
chuckled
giggled
snickered
tittered

moaned *(verb)*
"Oh no," moaned Ruth.
complained
grumbled
sighed
whined

spoke *(verb)*
"Set her free!" spoke the queen.
announced
declared
stated

quickly *(adverb)*
"Come on!" Jimmy said quickly.
hastily
hurriedly
rushedly
swiftly

slowly *(adverb)*
"I'm tired," Freya said slowly.
haltingly
lazily
leisurely
sluggishly

loudly *(adverb)*
"Don't!" Finn said loudly.
noisily
powerfully
thunderingly

quietly *(adverb)*
"Keep still," Kate said quietly.
faintly
gently
softly

Weather words

What's the weather like?

cloudy *(adjective)*
dull
gray
overcast

cold *(adjective)*
chilly
cool
bitter
bracing
nippy

foggy *(adjective)*
misty
hazy
murky

hot *(adjective)*
balmy
boiling
scorching
sweltering
tropical
warm

humid *(adjective)*
clammy
close
muggy
sultry

rainy *(adjective)*
damp
drizzly
pouring
showery
spitting
wet

stormy *(adjective)*
thundery

sunny *(adjective)*
bright
clear
cloudless
fine

windy *(adjective)*
blustery
breezy

Writing about the weather

The sun may...
shine
glare

Types of hot weather:
drought
heatwave

Rain may...
pour
teem
lash
pelt

Types of wet weather:
downpour
rain shower
sleet

Snow may...
drift
swirl
settle

Wind may...
batter
blast
blow
howl
roar

Types of windy weather:
breeze
gust
gale
tornado
whirlwind

Thunder may...
boom
crash
rumble

Types of stormy weather:
blizzard
hail
snowstorm
thunderstorm

Weather map symbols

Temperature is measured in degrees Fahrenheit (°F) or degrees Celsius (°C).

Wind speed and direction

Night words

night *(noun)*
The fox hunted in the **night**.

darkness
hours of darkness
nighttime
small hours

Animals that stay awake at night are nocturnal.

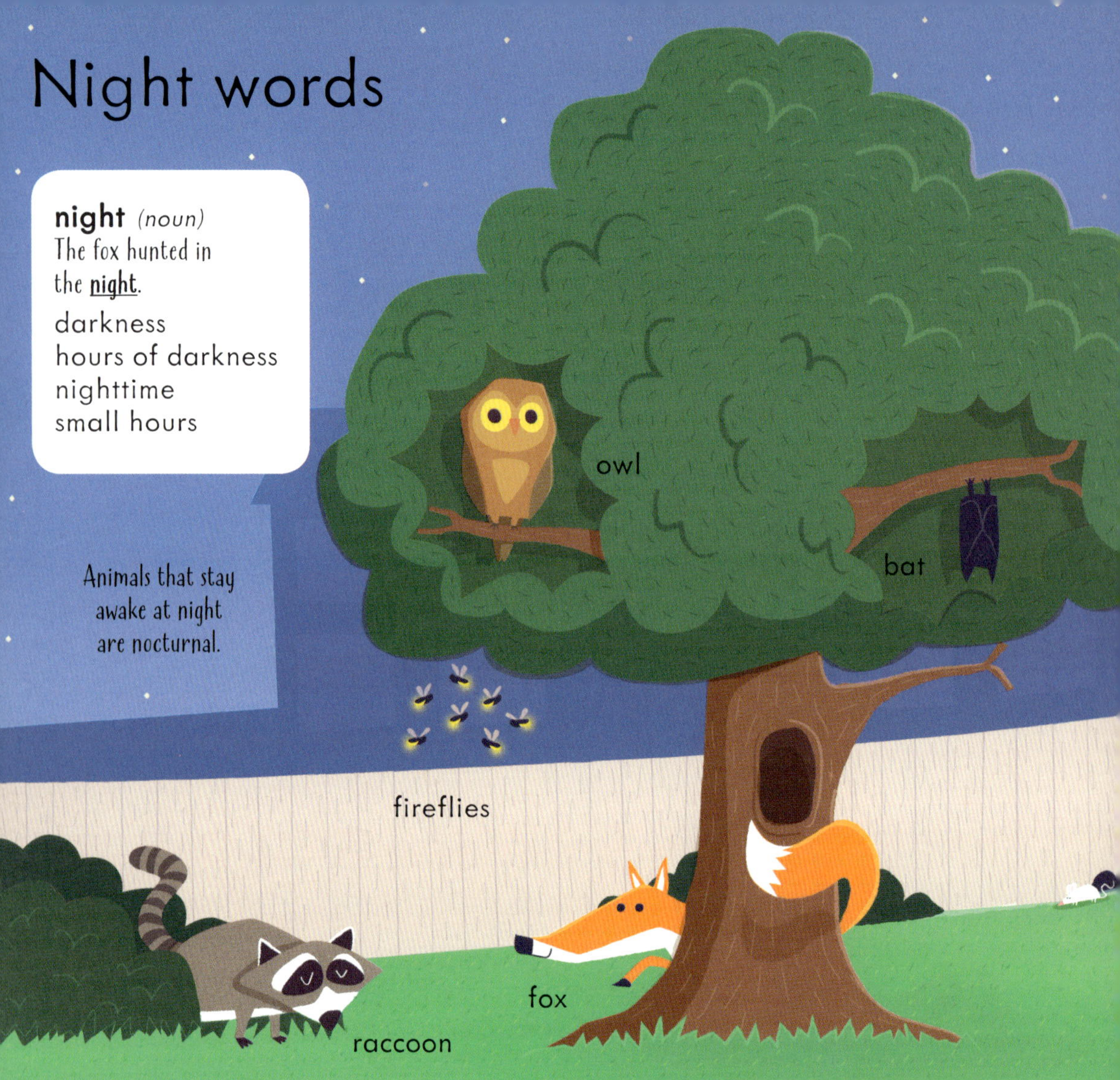

Describing night

dark *(adjective)*
An owl flew across a **dark** sky.

dusky
gloomy
inky
moonless
pitch-black
shadowy
starless

quiet *(adjective)*
The night was long and **quiet**.

silent
hushed
still

Night can also be...
moonlit
starry

Nighttime things

bed *(noun)*
Types of beds:
air
bunk
cot
crib
double
four-poster
futon
king-sized
queen
sofa

dream *(noun)*
I had a strange **dream** last night.

bad dream
nightmare

teddy bear *(noun)*
My **teddy bear's** name is Jumbo.

soft toy
stuffed animal
teddy

Describing people at night

afraid *(adjective)*
I'm **afraid** of the dark.

frightened
scared
terrified
petrified

asleep *(adjective)*
The baby was **asleep**.

fast asleep
napping
sleeping

awake *(adjective)*
It was midnight, but he was still **awake**.

wide-awake

tired *(adjective)*
The woman was so **tired**, she fell straight to sleep.

sleepy
exhausted
drowsy
weary
worn out

Things people do at night

lie *(verb)*
The lazy boy wanted to **lie** in bed all day.

laze
lounge
recline
sprawl

rest *(verb)*
It's late and I must **rest**.

have a rest
relax
take a nap

sleep *(verb)*
His uncle will **sleep** through anything.

doze
slumber
snooze

wake up *(verb)*
The bright light made them **wake up**.

get up
stir
wake

Story starters

The clock struck midnight as Fox began his nightly prowl...

Every house in the town was shrouded in darkness, except for one where a lamp still glowed...

Time words

time *(noun)*
The family went away for a long **time**.
period
spell
while

time *(verb)*
Can you **time** my swim please?
measure

clock *(noun)*
Types of clocks:
alarm clock
grandfather clock
hourglass

analogue clock

pocketwatch

digital clock

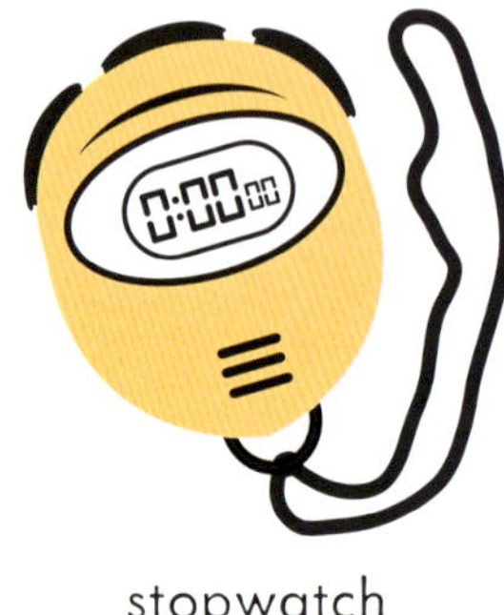
stopwatch

When?

day *(noun)*
Bats sleep during the **day**.
daylight
daytime

evening *(noun)*
Clouds gathered as **evening** approached.
dusk
sunset
twilight

finally *(adverb)*
Finally the ship arrived.
at last
eventually
in the end

immediately *(adverb)*
Let's leave **immediately**.
at once
now
promptly
right now
straightaway

moment *(noun)*
The guests will arrive in a **moment**.
instant
little while
second

morning *(noun)*
Is it **morning** yet?
dawn
sunrise

In what order?

first *(adverb)*
First the teacher stood up.
firstly
first of all

last *(adverb)*
The band played **last**.
at the end
last of all
lastly

next *(adverb)*
Who arrived **next**?
after that
afterwards
later
then

How often?

always *(adverb)*
That man is **always** on time.
consistently
forever
unfailingly

often *(adverb)*
That absent-minded girl is **often** late.
frequently
generally
regularly
usually

sometimes *(adverb)*
Everyone forgets **sometimes**.
occasionally
on occasion

Measurements and positions

How far? How much?

about *(adverb)*
The town is <u>about</u> a mile away.

approximately
around
nearly
roughly

almost *(adverb)*
An elephant weighs <u>almost</u> as much as 60 people.

nearly
just about

exactly *(adverb)*
The station is <u>exactly</u> a mile away.

precisely

fairly *(adverb)*
This bag is <u>fairly</u> heavy.

quite
rather
reasonably
somewhat

far *(adverb)*
The ship sailed <u>far</u>.

a long way
for miles

Where?

back *(noun)*
We always sit at the <u>back</u> of the bus.

end
far end
rear

faraway *(adjective)*
The captain explored <u>faraway</u> lands.

distant
farflung
remote

front *(noun)*
We reached the <u>front</u> of the line.

head
start

near *(preposition)*
I want to live <u>near</u> the sea.

close to
next to
not far from

opposite *(preposition)*
The boxer sat <u>opposite</u> his rival.

across from

place *(noun)*
Let's pitch the tent in a <u>place</u> that is safe and dry.

location
position
spot

measurements *(noun)*
Write down the room's <u>measurements</u>.

dimensions
length
size

height

width

Distance is measured in...
millimeters (mm)
centimeters (cm)
inches (in)
feet (ft)
yards (yd)
meters (m)
kilometers (km)
miles (mi)

Weight is measured in...
grams (g)
ounces (oz)
pounds (lb)
kilograms (kg)
tons (t)

The seasons

Spring

babies *(noun)*
Lots of animals have their <u>babies</u>.

young

build *(verb)*
Some birds <u>build</u> nests.

make
construct
put together

grow *(verb)*
Many plants start to <u>grow</u>.

get bigger
develop
shoot up

melt *(verb)*
The snow begins to <u>melt</u> as it gets warmer.

defrost
soften
thaw

blossom
nest

The first tulips open as the last daffodils are still in bloom.

tulips
daffodils

Summer

increase *(verb)*
The days <u>increase</u> in length.

get longer
expand
draw out

open *(verb)*
Many flowers start to <u>open</u>.

bloom
burst open

play *(verb)*
Children <u>play</u> outside.

have fun
play games

shrivel *(verb)*
Plants may <u>shrivel</u> in the heat.

droop
wilt
wither

umbrella
picnic hamper
lawn chair

Fall

decrease *(verb)*
The hours of daylight **decrease**.

get shorter
fall
dwindle

hang *(verb)*
The old branches **hang** low.

droop
bow
sag

fall *(verb)*
Leaves **fall** from the trees.

flutter down
swirl
tumble

mist *(noun)*
There's a **mist** in the air.

fog
haze

squirrel

toadstool

acorns

Snowflakes tumble gently through the air.

Winter

bear *(verb)*
Animals have to **bear** the cold weather.

put up with
suffer

cold *(adjective)*
In some places it gets very **cold**.

chilly
bracing
crisp
fresh
frosty
icy
nippy

cover *(verb)*
Snow may **cover** the ground.

blanket
carpet
hide
lie on

hard *(adjective)*
The ground freezes **hard**.

firm
rigid
solid

robin

icicle

snowman

snowdrift

In the town

town *(noun)*
Thousands of people live in the <u>town</u>.
city
metropolis

A town may be...
bustling
crowded
lively
overwhelming
throbbing

Sights and places

area *(noun)*
This part is a nice <u>area</u>.
place
district

restaurant *(noun)*
Which <u>restaurant</u> shall we go to?
café
coffee shop
bistro
pizzeria

street *(noun)*
Meet me at the end of the <u>street</u>!
avenue
boulevard
cul-de-sac
lane
road

Other sights and places:
art gallery
bridge
fountain
gym
hotel
ice rink
library
movie theater
museum
opera house
park
river
shopping center
mall
station
subway
swimming pool
theater
town square

Shopping

buy *(verb)*
Where did you <u>buy</u> those clothes?
get
pay for
purchase

line *(noun)*
The customers waited in a <u>line</u> to be served.
row

market *(noun)*
There are lots of stands at the <u>market</u>.
bazaar
fair
flea market
marketplace

money *(noun)*
Can you lend me some <u>money</u> to buy the book?
cash
coins

spend *(verb)*
How much money did you <u>spend</u>?
pay
splurge

store *(noun)*
Where's the nearest <u>store</u>, please?
boutique
corner shop
shop
supermarket
superstore

In the countryside

countryside *(noun)*
Let's go for a walk in the countryside.
country

Things you might see

bog *(noun)*
The ground is very wet near the bog.
marsh
marshland
swamp
wetlands

hill *(noun)*
Did you climb to the top of the hill?
hillside
mound

hole *(noun)*
The rambler twisted his ankle in the hole.
dip
hollow
pit
trench

hut *(noun)*
The woman lived in a lonely hut in the woods.
cabin
shack
shed
shelter

litter *(noun)*
They threw away their litter after the picnic.
trash
waste

notice *(noun)*
The notice says the field is flooded.
sign
bulletin

path *(noun)*
You must take the path around the lake.
lane
pathway
track
trail

post *(noun)*
Stay to the left of that post!
pillar
pole
stake

Other things:
orchard
windmill

River words

river *(noun)*
We had to wade through the river.
stream
creek
brook
rivulet

Rivers may...
babble
eddy
gush
meander
trickle

Parts of a river:
estuary (mouth of a river)
riverbank
source
waterfall
weir

Describing the countryside

calm *(adjective)*
It's so calm in the country.
peaceful
quiet
serene
tranquil

clean *(adjective)*
The water in the lake was ever so clean.
clear
fresh
pure
unpolluted

Farm words

farm *(noun)*
Types of farms:
arable farm (grows crops)
dairy farm (keeps cows)
livestock farm (keeps animals)
smallholding (a very small farm)

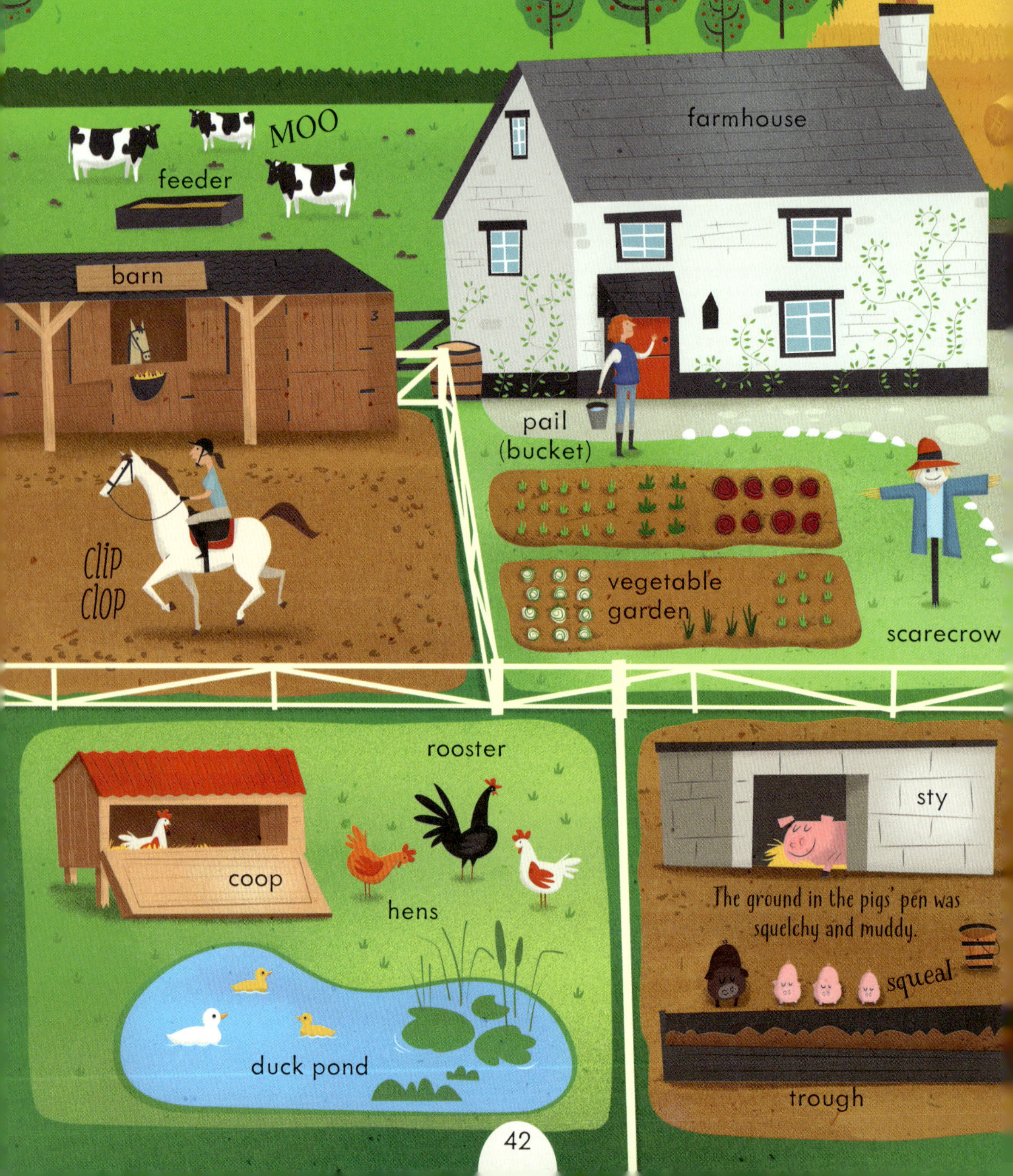

orchard

farmhouse

MOO

feeder

barn

pail (bucket)

clip clop

vegetable garden

scarecrow

field *(noun)*
The farmer is in the field.
meadow
paddock
pasture
plain

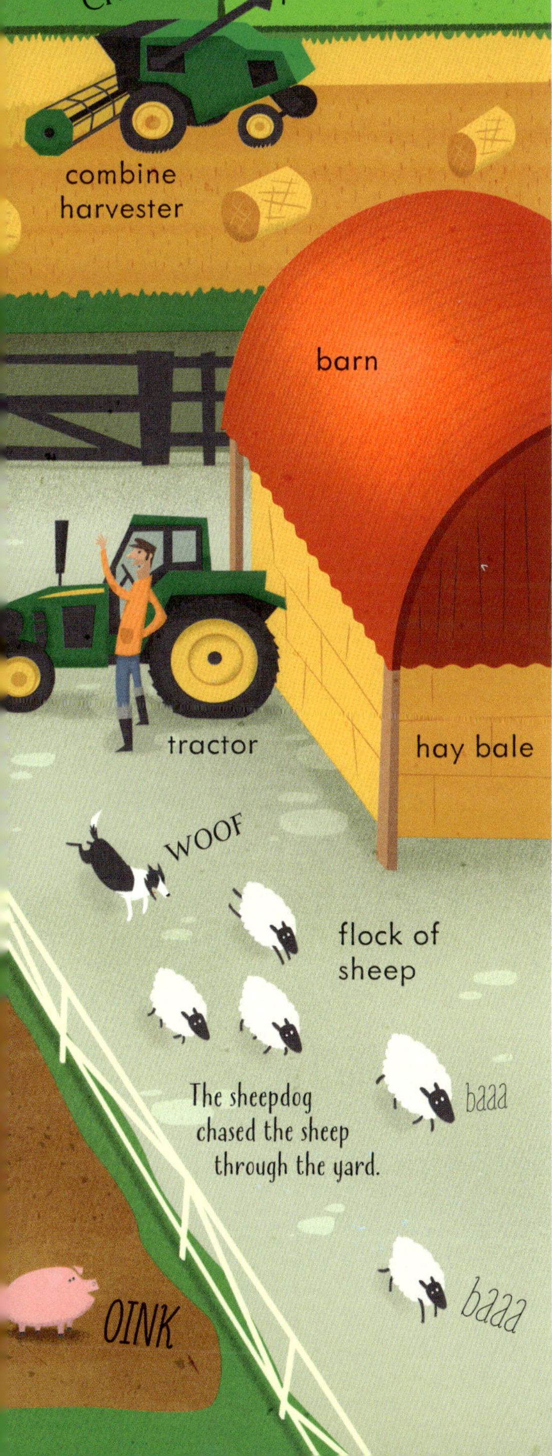

CHUG
CHUG
combine
harvester
barn
tractor
hay bale
WOOF
flock of
sheep
The sheepdog
chased the sheep
through the yard.
baaa
baaa
OINK

Writing about farms

even *(adjective)*
He raked the soil until it was even.
flat
level
smooth

keep *(verb)*
The farmers keep ducks on their farm.
care for
have
look after
tend

row *(noun)*
She planted a row of strawberry plants.
line

Farms grow...
barley
fruit
corn
oats
rice
sunflowers
vegetables
wheat

Describing farm animals

Types of cows:
Friesian
Hereford
Jersey

Types of pigs:
Mangalitza
Tamworth
Vietnamese pot-bellied

Types of horses:
carthorse
colt (young male)
filly (young female)

Horses may...
canter
gallop
jump
prance

Colors of horses:
bay
black
brown
chestnut
white

forelock
mane
bridle
saddle
muzzle
reins
hoof

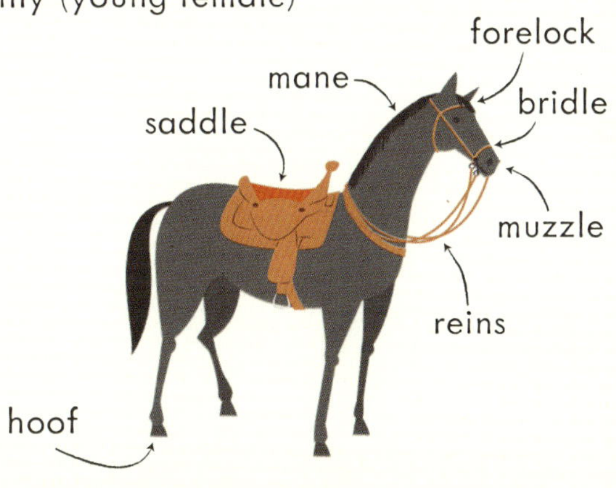

Seaside words

Places at the seaside

beach *(noun)*
Can we go to the **beach** today?
seashore
shore

port *(noun)*
Boats bobbed up and down in the **port**.
dock
harbor
marina

Other seaside places:
camping grounds
cliffs
amusement park
beach houses
hotel
pier
promenade
souvenir shop

Describing the seaside

busy *(adjective)*
The beach was **busy** with people.
crowded
heaving
packed

Beaches can be...
golden
muddy
pebbly
sandy
shingly
stony
windswept

Cliffs can be...
chalky
craggy
rocky

Things you might find on the beach:
beach ball
beach hut
bucket and shovel
beach chair
umbrella
sandcastle
windbreak

Seaside creatures

Tidepool creatures:
barnacle
hermit crab
sea anemone
sea urchin
shrimp
starfish

Seaside birds:
cormorant
petrel
guillemot
gull
tern
puffin

Things to do at the seaside

dip *(verb)*
We dared to **dip** our toes in the icy sea.
dunk
lower
plunge

swim *(verb)*
I want to **swim** in the sea.
go for a swim
go swimming
take a dip

Swimming strokes:
back stroke
breast stroke
butterfly
doggy paddle
front crawl

Other things to do:
crab fishing
explore tidepools
wade
sail
snorkel
sunbathe
surf

Things you might eat:
cotton candy
fish
ice cream
seafood

Hotel
boardwalk
wave
dinghy
The tide was coming in.
lighthouse
lifeguard
windsurfer
air mattress
yacht
kitesurfer
sandcastle
tidepools

Jungle words

jungle *(noun)*
The <u>jungle</u> is home to lots of animals.
rainforest
tropical forest

Describing jungles

dark *(adjective)*
It can be <u>dark</u> in a jungle.
gloomy
shady
shadowy

wet *(adjective)*
Jungles can be very <u>wet</u> places.
damp
dank
humid
moist
muggy

Writing about jungle plants

dangle *(verb)*
Vines <u>dangle</u> from the branches.
hang down
trail

thick *(adjective)*
Jungle plants are <u>thick</u> with leaves.
bushy
dense
leafy
lush
teeming

wind *(verb)*
Climbing plants <u>wind</u> around tree trunks.
twist
coil
loop
snake
wrap

Jungle plants:
palms
bamboo
lianas

Jungle explorers

climb *(verb)*
Explorers <u>climb</u> over rocks.
clamber
scramble

search *(verb)*
They <u>search</u> for things to eat.
hunt
look
seek
forage

Things jungle animals do

attack *(verb)*
Jaguars __attack__ their prey.
ambush
pounce on
strike at

chase *(verb)*
Tigers __chase__ other animals.
hunt
pursue
stalk
track

creep *(verb)*
Crocodiles __creep__ along the riverbank.
crawl
inch
scrabble

fly *(verb)*
Insects __fly__ up high.
flit
flutter
hover

hide *(verb)*
Creatures __hide__ in the shadows.
lie low
lurk
prowl
skulk

jump *(verb)*
Monkeys __jump__ between trees.
leap
swing

rush *(verb)*
Animals __rush__ to escape.
dart
dash
race
scuttle

wiggle *(verb)*
Snakes __wiggle__ along branches.
slither
slink
squirm
zigzag

In the mountains

dangerous *(adjective)*
It was a <u>dangerous</u> mountain to climb.
hazardous
precarious
risky
treacherous

high *(adjective)*
The <u>high</u> mountain touched the clouds.
lofty
soaring
towering

Mountains can also be...
craggy
forest-fringed
misty
rocky
rugged
sheer

Things to do in the mountains:
climb
hike
ski
snowboard
sled
trek

In the desert

bright *(adjective)*
A bright sun shone in the sky.
blazing
dazzling
fiery
glaring
scorching

dry *(adjective)*
The desert is a dry place.
arid
bone dry
dusty
parched
sandy

hot *(adjective)*
It's hot at noon.
boiling hot
sweltering
searing
blistering

spiky *(adjective)*
He pricked his thumb on a spiky cactus.
spiny
prickly
thorny

Under the sea

catch *(verb)*
He tried to <u>catch</u> fish.
capture
net
snare
trap

diver *(noun)*
A <u>diver</u> wears a wetsuit.
deepsea diver
frogman

flick *(verb)*
Fish <u>flick</u> their tail fins.
swish
waggle
wave

salty *(adjective)*
The water is <u>salty</u>.
briny
brackish

seabed *(noun)*
A lobster scuttled along the <u>seabed</u>.
bottom of the ocean
ocean floor
sea floor

sink *(verb)*
The anchor began to <u>sink</u>.
drop
go down
plummet
plunge

underwater *(adjective)*
The old boat is <u>underwater</u>.
submerged

Story endings

By the time the cloud of sand had cleared, the giant squid had disappeared.

Desperate for air, she snatched the pearl from the clam and swam to the surface.

Would anyone ever explore this city under the sea again?

Under the ground

centipedes

worms

mole

nest *(noun)*
An animal sleeps in its nest.

burrow
den

mud *(noun)*
The mole dug in the mud.

dirt
earth
soil

roots

pipe

rat

sewer

Describing things underground

deep *(adjective)*
The deep pit went on and on.

bottomless
cavernous
gaping

hard *(adjective)*
A machine cut through the hard earth.

firm
solid
tough

old *(adjective)*
There are old remains deep underground.

ancient
aged
prehistoric

smelly *(adjective)*
It was pitch black in the smelly, clammy sewer.

stinking
rank
reeking
fetid

In the air

air *(noun)*
The balloon soared into the **air**.
atmosphere
sky

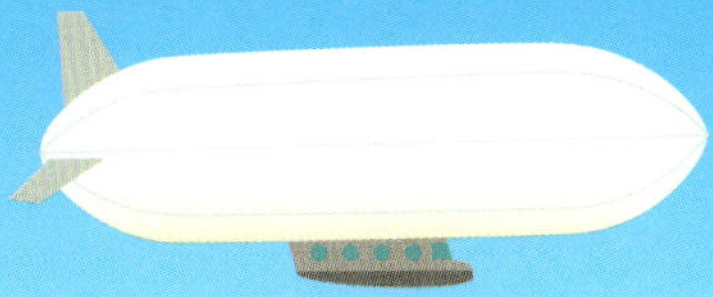

basket
hot-air balloon
glider
kite
rotor
helicopter
airship
parachute
hang glider

plane *(noun)*
The **plane** was ready to land.
airplane
aircraft
jet

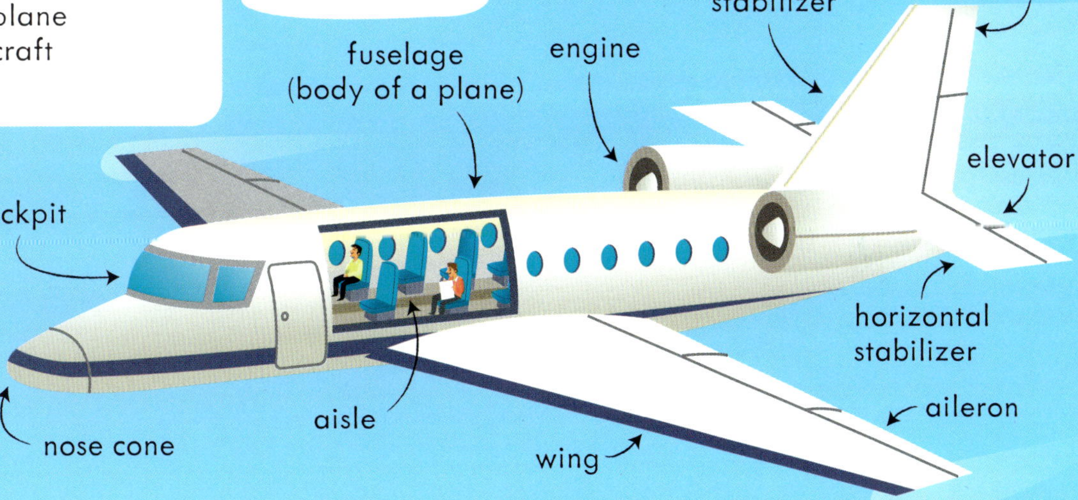

vertical stabilizer
rudder
fuselage (body of a plane)
engine
elevator
cockpit
horizontal stabilizer
aileron
aisle
nose cone
wing

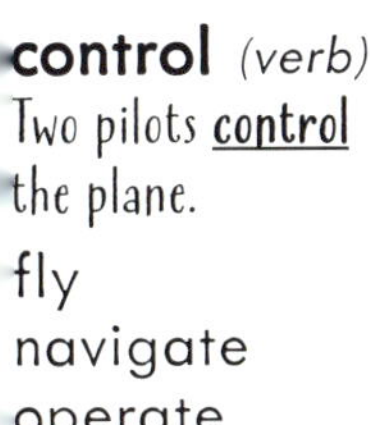

control *(verb)*
Two pilots **control** the plane.
fly
navigate
operate
pilot

glide *(verb)*
See how they **glide** through the air.
drift
float
hover
sail

rise *(verb)*
The plane will steadily **rise**.
go up
climb
ascend
soar
rocket

type *(noun)*
Every **type** of aircraft was at the airshow.
kind
sort
variety

Boat words

boat *(noun)*
They sailed the <u>boat</u> around the island.

ship
craft
vessel

Types of boats:
aircraft carrier
barge
battleship
canoe
catamaran
container ship
cruise liner
dinghy
ferry
fishing boat
galleon
gondola
hovercraft
kayak
lifeboat
motorboat
narrow boat
punt
raft
rowboat
sailboat
speedboat
tanker
trawler
tug
yacht

People out on deck watched whales dive and splash.

bridge
ship's wheel
bow (front of a boat)
lifejackets
anchor

The two-hulled catamaran sailed quickly through the water.

A container ship carried its heavy cargo across the ocean.
Boats can...
bob up and down
capsize
cruise
dock
drift
float
glide
heave
plow through the water
rock from side to side
sail
set sail
speed
steam ahead
funnel
lifeboats
porthole
hull (body of a boat)
stern (back of a boat)
buoy
propeller
6
yacht
rudder
keel
oar
A motorboat zipped through the water leaving a trail of foam.
The rower held a steady path through the water.

On the road

road *(noun)*
street
lane
avenue
highway
route
track

car *(noun)*
automobile
motor
vehicle

drive *(verb)*
It's hard to **drive** this truck.
maneuver
operate
steer

truck *(noun)*
semi
tanker

traffic jam *(noun)*
They're stuck in a **traffic jam**.
bottleneck
gridlock
hold up

start *(verb)*
The driver tried to **start** the engine.
activate
fire up
switch on
turn on

stop *(verb)*
They had to **stop** suddenly.
brake
slow down
halt
decelerate

speed *(verb)*
The motorcycles **speed** around the corner.
accelerate
tear
zip
zoom

fast *(adjective)*
She drove a **fast** car.
quick
speedy
swift
powerful

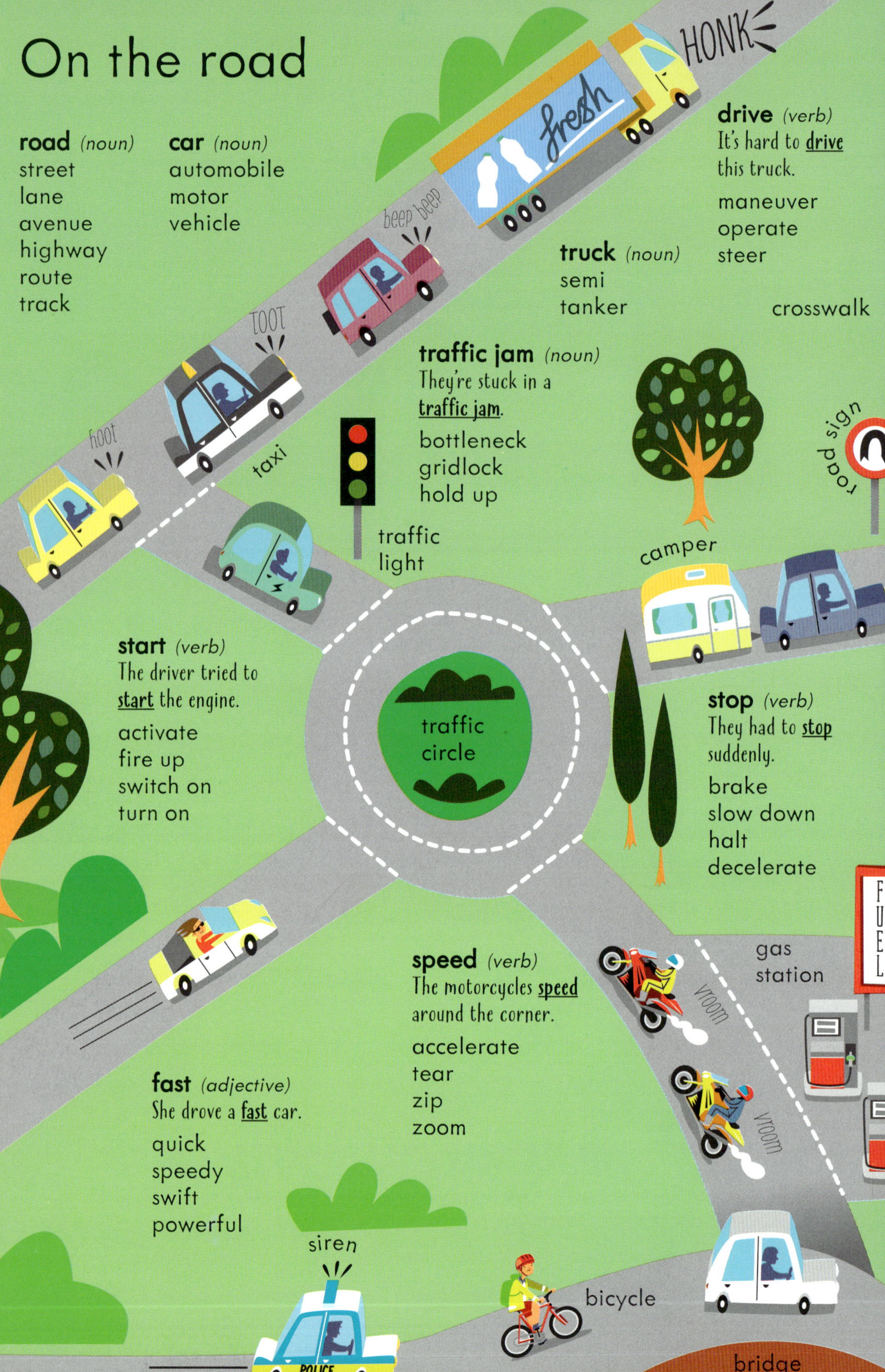

sports car
tandem
electric car
cycle lane
tunnel
sleek (adjective)
The car had such a sleek body.
aerodynamic
streamlined
skid (verb)
The driver tried not to skid.
slip
slide
spin
squeak (verb)
Do my car's brakes squeak?
screech
squeal
broken (adjective)
The broken car wouldn't start.
broken-down
conked out
busted
P
pothole
junction
intersection
swerve (verb)
The van had to swerve to the left.
veer
dodge
WHEEE
RV
dumpster
traffic cones
construction
backhoe
stretch limo
pfft
pfft
crash into (verb)
Two cars crash into each other.
bump into
collide with
crawl (verb)
The cars crawl along.
creep
inch
SUV
tractor
slow (adjective)
The slow tractor held up the traffic.
dawdling
slow-moving
accident (noun)
There was an accident at the intersection.
crash
collision
BANG

Travel words

departure board

train *(noun)*
engine
locomotive

Types of trains:
diesel train
electric train
freight train
high-speed train
maglev
monorail
steam train
underground train

Trains...
clank
depart
grind to a halt
hurtle
pull into a station
trundle
whistle

FWEE FWEE

The guard blows two short blasts on his whistle.

cancel *(verb)*
We must <u>cancel</u> the train because of the deep snow.
call off
scrap

country *(noun)*
The boat sailed from one <u>country</u> to another.
land

delay *(verb)*
The airline had to <u>delay</u> the flight.
postpone
suspend

journey *(noun)*
Where did your <u>journey</u> take you?
excursion
expedition
tour
travels
trek
trip
voyage

late *(adjective)*
The driver was <u>late</u>.
behind schedule
delayed
not on time

luggage *(noun)*
The man put his <u>luggage</u> in the compartment.
bag
case
baggage
backpack
suitcase
rolling luggage

overseas *(adverb)*
The family often goes <u>overseas</u> all summer.
abroad

prepare *(verb)*
Did you <u>prepare</u> for the trip?
get ready
make plans
plan
train

ready *(adjective)*
Everything was <u>ready</u> for the journey.
arranged
organized
prepared
set up

Passengers sit patiently on board waiting for the train to depart.

People stride up and down the platform.

squeeze *(verb)*
She tried to <u>squeeze</u> a second sweater into her bag.

cram
pack
stuff

travel *(verb)*
My brother loves to <u>travel</u>.

go on trips
see the world
tour

While traveling you may feel...
excited
fidgety
jet-lagged
nervous
seasick
travel-sick

Items to pack:
book
map
passport
phrase book
snacks
ticket

Bike words

bike *(noun)*
bicycle
cycle

Types of bikes:
folding bike
mountain bike
road bike
tandem
tricycle
unicycle

Story starter and ending

"Your prize is a plane ticket to anywhere in the world..."

Unpacking their cases they agreed it couldn't have been a better trip.

Feeling sick

behave *(verb)*
His fever made the man behave oddly.
act

bump *(verb)*
What did you bump your knee on?
bang
knock
hit
injure
strike

catch *(verb)*
How did the patient catch a cold?
get
develop
contract
pick up

cut *(verb)*
When did the chef cut her finger?
graze
nick
sever
slash

different *(adjective)*
The patient has different symptoms.
mixed
various

dizzy *(adjective)*
The girl felt dizzy.
faint
light-headed
shaky
wobbly
woozy

doctor *(noun)*
Can I see a doctor?
medic
physician

Types of doctors:
specialist
GP (general practitioner)
surgeon

health *(noun)*
Walking is good for your health.
fitness
wellbeing

hurt *(verb)*
How did you hurt your leg?
harm
injure
wound

ill *(adjective)*
Are you still ill?
unwell
poorly
out of sorts
sick

illness *(noun)*
The doctor diagnosed her illness.
sickness
bug
disease
infection
ailment
virus

itch *(verb)*
The rash made his skin itch.
prickle
tingle

loose *(adjective)*
The boy had a loose front tooth.
wiggly

lump *(noun)*
There's a strange lump on his arm.
bump
bulge
swelling

medicine *(noun)*
The doctor prescribed this medicine.
drug
medication
remedy

Types of medicine:
antibiotic
cream
injection/shot
lotion
ointment
painkiller
pill
spray
tablet

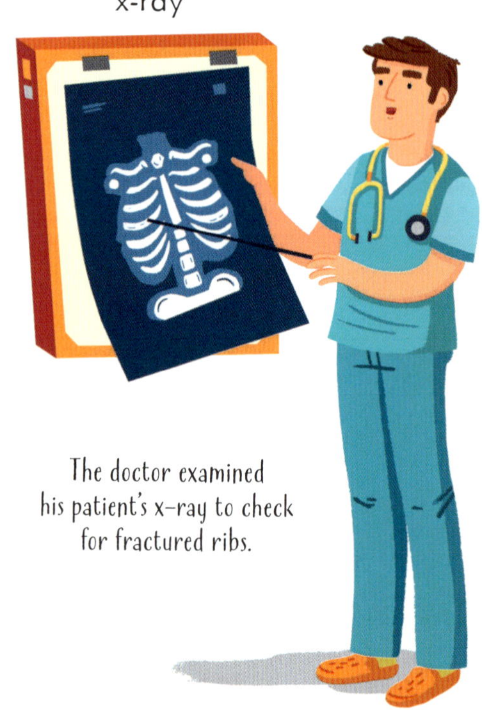

The doctor examined his patient's x-ray to check for fractured ribs.

pain *(noun)*
She felt a slight pain in her back.

ache
cramp
discomfort
soreness
twinge

pale *(adjective)*
His skin looks pale.

pasty
ashen
sickly

problem *(noun)*
What is the problem?

difficulty
trouble
predicament

recover *(verb)*
You will recover in a week or so.

get better
get well
heal
improve
recuperate

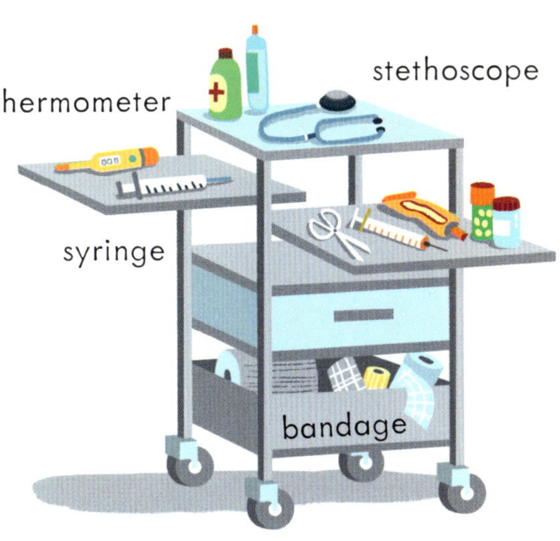

serious *(adjective)*
The old man had a serious illness.

critical
grave
major

sick *(adjective)*
I felt sick on the train.

unwell
ill
nauseous
queasy
green

soothe *(verb)*
The nurse tried to soothe his patient.

calm
comfort
reassure

sore *(adjective)*
The young woman's leg was really sore.

aching
bruised
hurting
painful
tender

take care of *(verb)*
They'll take care of you.

care for
look after
treat

weak *(adjective)*
My great uncle feels weak after his operation.

delicate
feeble
frail

well *(adjective)*
When will he be well again?

fit
healthy
in good health

wheeze *(verb)*
She suddenly started to wheeze.

breathe heavily
gasp
pant

worry *(verb)*
You'll feel better if you don't worry.

fret
fuss
get worked up

Buildings

building *(noun)*
house
apartment
building

Types of buildings:
factory
garage
hospital
hotel
mill
museum
office tower
palace
power station
prison
skyscraper
station
theater
church

Describing buildings

Buildings can be made of...
brick
concrete
glass
marble
steel
stone
timber

Buildings can be...
crumbling
futuristic
gleaming
imposing
lofty
ornate
towering

helipad

Glistening towers of glass and steel stood shoulder to shoulder along the horizon.

roof garden

balcony

Building things

brick *(noun)*
Each **brick** was made of stone.
block
slab

build *(verb)*
It took ten years to **build** the castle.
construct
erect
put up

crack *(noun)*
There was a **crack** in the wall.
gap
hole

dig *(verb)*
The builders **dig** a huge hole for the foundations.
excavate

join *(verb)*
The plumbers **join** the pipes together.
attach
connect
fasten
fix

lump *(noun)*
He added the concrete in a **lump**.
blob
dollop
splotch

make *(verb)*
How did they **make** the plaster?
form
shape
mold

pile *(noun)*
They put the bags in a **pile**.
heap
mound
stack

plan *(noun)*
They studied the **plan** before they began building.
design
diagram
drawing
sketch

pulley

cut *(verb)*
They had to **cut** the planks in half.
chop
divide
saw

layer *(noun)*
The walls need another **layer** of paint.
coat
covering

piece *(noun)*
They built the tower **piece** by **piece**.
bit
part
section

size *(noun)*
She cut the boards to the right **size**.
measurements
dimensions
height
length
breadth
width

scaffolding

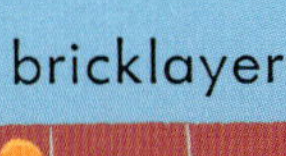

concrete mixer

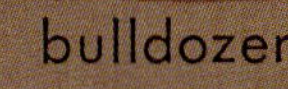

Around the house

house *(noun)*
home
abode
dwelling

Types of houses:
bungalow
cabin
cottage
detached house
mansion
semi-detached house
terraced house
villa

Other places where people live:
apartment
condo
recreational vehicle
townhouse
houseboat
loft
tour bus

Inside a house

chair *(noun)*
seat

Types of chairs:
armchair
bench
dining chair
rocking chair
stool

Types of furniture:
bookcase
cabinet
coffee table
desk
dining table
shelf
dresser

On the floors:
carpet
wooden flooring
rugs
tile

On the walls:
paint
tile
wallpaper
wood paneling

Describing a house

chilly *(adjective)*
It was <u>chilly</u> in their loft.

cold
airy
drafty

cozy *(adjective)*
The cottage is <u>cozy</u>.

comfortable
comfy
snug
warm

mess *(noun)*
Clean up the <u>mess</u>!

clutter
jumble

messy *(adjective)*
Her bungalow was always <u>messy</u>.

dusty
untidy

neat *(adjective)*
The boy kept his room <u>neat</u>.

clean
spick-and-span
tidy
uncluttered

Things people do inside a house

clean *(verb)*
We need to <u>clean</u> every room.

wash
polish
scrub
spring-clean
sweep
brush
vacuum
dust
wipe

close *(verb)*
Can you <u>close</u> the curtains, please?

shut
pull
draw

decorate *(verb)*
I want to <u>decorate</u> the walls.

paint
wallpaper

Clothes words

clothes *(noun)*
attire
clothing
costume
outfit

bag *(noun)*
backpack
handbag
duffle bag
messenger bag
shoulder bag

coat *(noun)*
anorak
duffle coat
jacket
parka
raincoat
trench coat

dress *(noun)*
ball gown
formal dress
mini dress
party dress
prom dress
sari
sundress
wedding dress

hat *(noun)*
baseball cap
beanie
beret
bowler hat
cowboy hat
fedora
fez
sombrero
stocking cap
top hat

jacket *(noun)*
blazer
bomber jacket
denim jacket
tuxedo

shoes *(noun)*
ankle boots
athletic shoes
ballet flats
boots
cowboy boots
flip flops
heels
sandals
slippers
stilettos
tennis shoes
hiking boots
rain boots

skirt *(noun)*
kilt
miniskirt

suit *(noun)*
boiler suit
lounge suit
three-piece suit
tracksuit
dress suit

top *(noun)*
blouse
cardigan
fleece
polo shirt
pullover
sweater
sweatshirt
tanktop
T-shirt
vest

pants *(noun)*
capris
flare leg
jeans
leggings
skinny jeans
slacks
shorts

And...
bathrobe
bow tie
gloves
kimono
nightshirt
panties
pajamas
scarf
boxer shorts
suspenders
tie
underwear

Writing about clothes

dirty *(adjective)*
My clothes are **dirty** because I've been gardening.
grubby
mucky
muddy

fashion *(noun)*
They followed the latest **fashion**.
look
style
trend

fashionable *(adjective)*
You always wear such **fashionable** outfits.
stylish
trendy

loose *(adjective)*
She likes to wear **loose** shirts.
baggy
roomy

neat *(adjective)*
You look very **neat** in your suit.
polished
groomed
tidy

scruffy *(adjective)*
That old dress is very **scruffy**.
messy
shabby
ragged
tattered

stain *(noun)*
There was a grease **stain** on his shirt.
mark
spot

tight *(adjective)*
Are my skinny jeans too **tight**?
clingy
fitted
tight-fitting

Clothes can also be...
casual
elegant
formal
frilly

Getting dressed words

bare *(adjective)*
The baby was **bare** except for his diaper.
naked
nude
undressed

take off *(verb)*
He had to **take off** his wet jeans.
remove

tie *(verb)*
The girl struggled to **tie** her shoes.
do up
fasten
lace

undo *(verb)*
I can't **undo** my pants.
loosen
open
unbutton
untie
unzip

wear *(verb)*
What clothes are you going to **wear**?
put on

fabric *(noun)*
The shirt was made from an unusual **fabric**.
cloth
material

Types of fabric...
chintz
corduroy
cotton
lace
linen
satin
silk
taffeta
velour
velvet

pattern *(noun)*
I like the bird **pattern** on your T-shirt.
design
decoration
motif

Food words

food *(noun)*
grub
nourishment

drink *(noun)*
What <u>drink</u> would you like?
beverage
refreshment

drink *(verb)*
Please <u>drink</u> the rest of the juice.
gulp
guzzle
sip

eat *(verb)*
Don't <u>eat</u> that!
bite
chew
chomp
devour
gobble
munch
nibble
scarf
swallow

meal *(noun)*
That <u>meal</u> was delicious.
banquet
buffet
feast
picnic

dessert *(noun)*
What <u>dessert</u> do you want?
sweet dish
treat

fruit *(noun)*
Types of fruit:
apple
apricot
avocado
banana
blackberry
blackcurrant
blueberry
cherry
clementine
date
fig
gooseberry
grapes
grapefruit
greengage
kiwi fruit
lemon
lime
lychee
mandarin
mango
melon
nectarine
orange
papaya
peach
pear
pineapple
plum
pomegranate
raspberry
rhubarb
satsuma
star fruit
strawberry
tomato

juicy watermelon

meat *(noun)*
Types of meat:
bacon
beef
bison
burger
chicken
chorizo
duck
goose
ham
lamb
mutton
pheasant
pork
sausage
steak
turkey
venison

vegetable
(noun)
greens
Types of vegetables:
artichoke
asparagus
beets
broccoli
cabbage
carrot
cauliflower
celery
corn
eggplant
fava beans
garlic
green onion
leek
lettuce
mushroom
onion
parsnip
peas
pepper
potato
pumpkin
radish
snow peas
spinach
squash
turnip
zucchini

Types of spices:
cayenne
cinnamon
cloves
cumin
chili
nutmeg
paprika
turmeric
vanilla

Types of herbs:
basil
bay leaves
cilantro
parsley
rosemary
sage
thyme

bread *(noun)*
Types of bread:
bagel
baguette
biscuit
bread stick
loaf
pita
roll
tortilla

seafood *(noun)*
Types of seafood:
catfish
cod
clams
crab
halibut
mackerel
pollock
salmon
sardine
sea bass
shrimp
tilapia
trout
tuna

Describing food

bitter *(adjective)*
The bitter drink made my lips pucker.
sharp
sour
tart

disgusting *(adjective)*
Yuck. This hot dog is disgusting.
foul
revolting
vile

full of *(adjective)*
The loaf is full of raisins.
filled with
stuffed with
packed with
crammed with

greasy *(adjective)*
The stew is rather greasy.
fatty
oily

hot *(adjective)*
Eat carefully! The pizza is hot.
piping hot
sizzling

mild *(adjective)*
I can't taste the garlic. It's too mild.
bland
delicate
faint
subtle

raw *(adjective)*
The beef is raw.
bloody
underdone
uncooked

spicy *(adjective)*
Did you find the sauce too spicy?
hot
peppery

stale *(adjective)*
The man said the bread was stale.
moldy
past its best

sweet *(adjective)*
The icing on the cake is too sweet.
sugary

taste *(noun)*
This cheese has a strange taste.
flavor
tang

taste *(verb)*
Could you taste the sauce?
sample
sip
test
try

tasty *(adjective)*
I've never had such a tasty truffle.
delicious
appetizing
mouthwatering
scrumptious
yummy

thick *(adjective)*
The custard is thick.
lumpy
congealed
stiff

thin *(adjective)*
The soup is thin.
runny
watery

Food can also be...
buttery
chewy
creamy
crisp
crumbly
crunchy
flavorless
fluffy
gooey
juicy
leathery
mushy
nourishing
plain
rich
salty
seasoned
sloppy
soft
spongy
sticky
succulent
sweet-and-sour
tender
tough
vinegary
zesty
zingy

Cooking

ladle
colander
sieve
spatula

amount *(noun)*
What **amount** of butter is required?
quantity

cook *(verb)*
Who wants to **cook** lunch?
make
prepare
put together

cool *(verb)*
Cool the melted butter before adding.
chill
refrigerate

difficult *(adjective)*
The recipe for puff pastry is **difficult**.
hard
complicated
complex
tricky

dollop *(noun)*
Add a **dollop** of batter to the pan.
drop
lump

cup *(noun)*
Types of cups:
glass
goblet
mug
stemware
tumbler

easy *(adjective)*
It's an **easy** recipe.
simple
straightforward
uncomplicated

extra *(adjective)*
I think that it needs **extra** seasoning.
more
further
additional

fill *(verb)*
Can you **fill** the pitcher with milk?
refill
replenish
top up

heat *(verb)*
Heat the milk gently in a pan.
warm up

instructions *(noun)*
Follow the **instructions** in the recipe.
directions

main *(adjective)*
The **main** ingredient is rice.
chief
key
major

mash *(verb)*
Mash the potatoes with a fork.
crush
pound
pulp

organize *(verb)*
Who will **organize** the dinner?
arrange
plan
prepare
set up

pour *(verb)*
Pour the water into the flour.
add
tip

serve *(verb)*
Would you **serve** the carrots, please?
dish up
pass around

stir *(verb)*
Stir the eggs together first.
beat
whip
whisk

When people cook, they may...
bake
barbecue
boil
fry
grill
poach
roast
sauté
scramble
steam
stir-fry

box *(noun)*
carton
container
package

Fun and hobbies

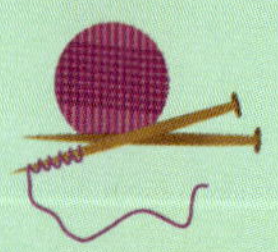

book *(noun)*
Types of books:
atlas
dictionary
encyclopedia
novel
picture book
reference book
story book
textbook
thesaurus

club *(noun)*
The drama club has over fifty members.
group
society

computer *(noun)*
Types of computers:
laptop
PC
tablet

diary *(noun)*
Do you like to keep a diary?
journal
record

draw *(verb)*
I want to draw another picture.
sketch
doodle

exhibition *(noun)*
My painting is in the exhibition.
display
show

fun *(noun)*
What do you do for fun?
entertainment
pleasure
recreation

hobby *(noun)*
Cooking is my hobby of choice.
activity
interest
pastime

Some hobbies:
acting
bird watching
cooking
dancing
fishing
football
gardening
knitting
origami
painting
photography
reading
sewing

movie *(noun)*
The movie was too long.
film

Types of movies:
action movie
adventure movie
cartoon
comedy
drama
horror movie
romance
sci-fi
thriller
Western

party *(noun)*
Did you enjoy the party?
celebration
gathering
reception

photo *(noun)*
The best photo won a prize.
photograph
picture
snapshot

picture *(noun)*
That's a good picture.
drawing
painting
landscape
portrait
cartoon
sketch

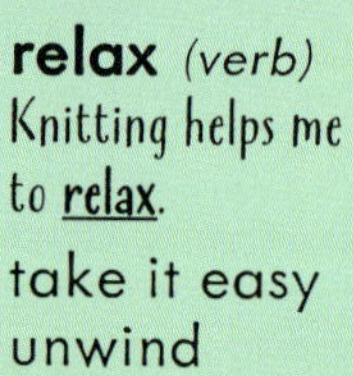

relax *(verb)*
Knitting helps me to relax.
take it easy
unwind

story *(noun)*
It's soothing to read a story before bed.
tale

Types of stories:
adventure story
detective story
fairy tale
fantasy story
ghost story
mystery

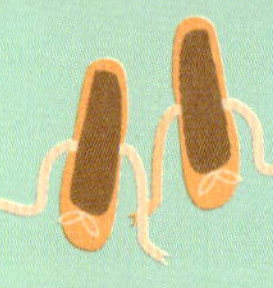

Job words

job *(noun)*
career
occupation
profession

doctor

pilot

artist

vet

builder

architect

scientist

hairdresser

waiter

firefighter

mechanic

gardener

dentist

nurse

photographer

farmer

chef

receptionist

Other jobs:
accountant
beautician
butcher
carpenter
designer
electrician
engineer
journalist
lawyer
librarian
musician
pharmacist
plumber
police officer
real estate agent
secretary
store owner
social worker
teacher
zookeeper

boss *(noun)*
His boss said the man was always late.
director
manager
supervisor

inspect *(verb)*
An official came to inspect their work.
check
examine
investigate
monitor
survey
study

unemployed *(adjective)*
She had been unemployed for a month.
out of a job
out of work

work *(noun)*
Building is hard work.
labor
toil

work *(verb)*
My sisters work in a bank.
have a job
earn a living
go to work

Sports words

sport *(noun)*
exercise

Types of sports:
archery
badminton
baseball
basketball
boxing
cycling
diving
football
golf
gymnastics
hockey
ice hockey
judo
karate
netball
pool
rowing
rugby
running
skating
skiing
soccer
squash
swimming
table tennis
tennis
volleyball

Sports venues:
arena
court
field
ice rink
ring
stadium
swimming pool
track

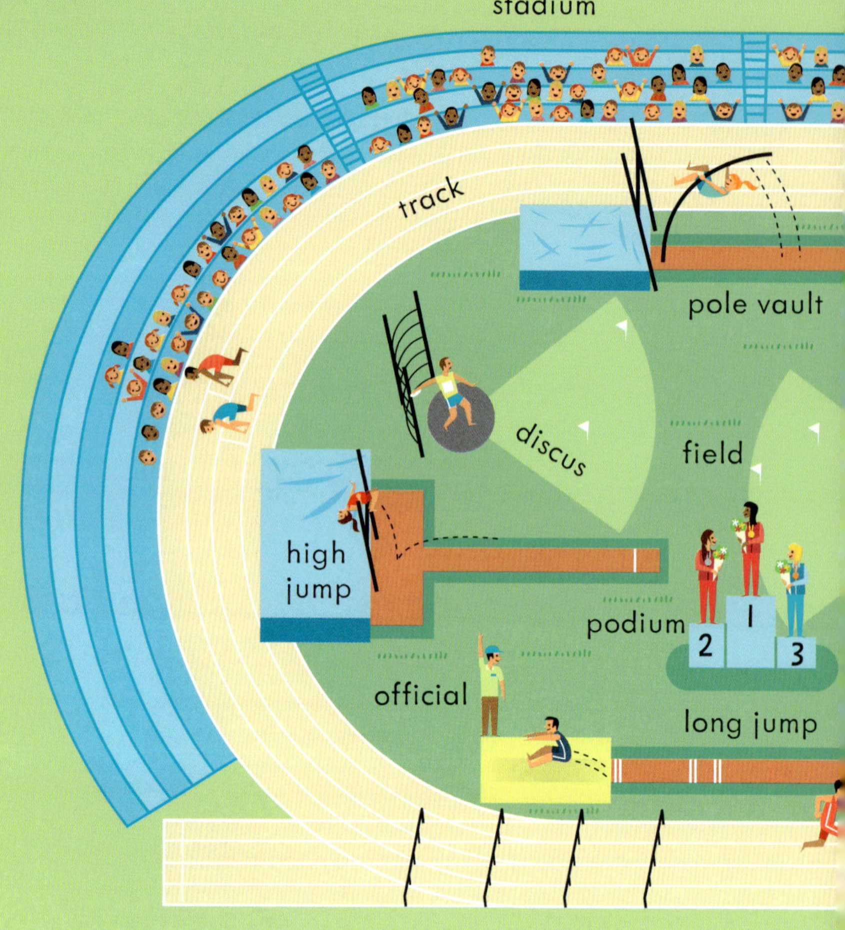

Describing athletes

athlete *(noun)*
Which **athlete** will win?
competitor
contestant
participant
player
runner
sportsman
sportswoman
swimmer

best *(adjective)*
The **best** runner won the race.
finest
top

skill *(noun)*
The high jumper showed such **skill**.
ability
talent

sporty *(adjective)*
She had always been very **sporty**.
athletic
energetic
fit

winner *(noun)*
The **winner** took the trophy.
champion
victor

medals

Things athletes do

beat *(verb)*
I will **beat** the others.
defeat
thrash

cheat *(verb)*
Please don't **cheat**.
break the rules

dive *(verb)*
He tried to **dive** for the ball.
lunge

hit *(verb)*
Try to **hit** the ball with your racket.
knock
strike
tap
touch

kick *(verb)*
Can you **kick** the ball?
dribble
pass

lift *(verb)*
Let's **lift** him up so he can catch the ball.
hoist
raise

lose *(verb)*
They will **lose** again.
be beaten
be defeated
suffer defeat

play *(verb)*
The team will **play** their rivals.
challenge
play against
take on

At the circus

amuse *(verb)*
The strongmen amuse the crowds.
delight
entertain

face *(noun)*
Look at the acrobat's concentrated face.
expression

joke *(noun)*
Her joke was funnier than his.
gag
pun

laugh *(verb)*
The show made us laugh.
chuckle
giggle
chortle
snicker
titter

tease *(verb)*
The clowns tease each other.
laugh at
make fun of

trick *(noun)*
His trick was astonishing.
stunt

Circus acts...
do magic tricks
perform
take a bow

Dance words

dance *(verb)*
Shall we <u>dance</u>?

boogie
bop
move to the music
sway to the beat

Line dancers move in time together.

Ballet dancers are graceful and light on their feet.

A street dancer balances on one hand.

People who dance together are each other's partners.

The flamenco dancer's frilly dress swishes from side to side.

spin *(verb)*
The dancer could **spin** on one foot.

go around
turn
twirl
twist
pirouette

Dancers may...

glide
gyrate
jiggle
prance
shuffle
stomp
swing
wiggle

Dancers can be...

agile
balletic
elegant
graceful
lithe
nimble
sprightly

Music

group *(noun)*
What's your favorite **group**?

act
band
choir
orchestra

musician *(noun)*
Each **musician** in the band played a different instrument.

performer
player

Types of musicians:
cellist
drummer
fiddler
flautist
guitarist
organist
pianist
soloist
trumpeter
violinist

Things musicians do

fade *(verb)*
The sound of the choir began to **fade**.

diminish
disappear
dwindle
grow faint
wane

perform *(verb)*
The orchestra will **perform** after the interval.

play
appear

practice *(verb)*
The violinist had to **practice** her solo.

rehearse
go over
prepare
fine tune

Song words

sing *(verb)*
Her mother would always **sing** at parties.

serenade
warble

singer *(noun)*
Who is the lead **singer**?

vocalist

Types of singers:
alto
baritone
bass
soprano
tenor
treble

song *(noun)*
What **song** are you singing?

ditty
melody
tune

Describing music and musicians

Styles of music:
country
folk
hip hop
jazz
musical
opera
pop
rap
reggae
rhythm and blues
rock

clear *(adjective)*
The tenor has such a **clear** voice.

distinct
audible
recognizable

famous *(adjective)*
Have you heard of that **famous** pianist?

celebrated
renowned
well-known
world-famous

Music can be...
catchy
classical
dramatic
enchanting
haunting
improvised
joyful
repetitive
rousing
rhythmic
shrill
tuneful

Musical instruments

A large group of musicians play together in an orchestra.

A conductor helps an orchestra play together.

String instruments
cello
double bass
guitar
harp
sitar
ukulele
viola
violin

Brass instruments
bugle
cornet
euphonium
french horn
trombone
trumpet
tuba

Wind instruments
bagpipes
bassoon
clarinet
flute
harmonica
oboe
recorder
saxophone

Percussion instruments
bass drum
chimes
cymbals
glockenspiel
kettle drum
triangle
wood block
xylophone

Keyboard instruments
accordion
electric organ
harpsichord
piano
organ
synthesizer

Science lab

drip *(verb)*
Liquid began to **drip**.
dribble
leak
ooze
trickle

effect *(noun)*
What **effect** will heat have on the metal?
consequence
result

happen *(verb)*
What will **happen** if you add water?
come about
occur
take place

invent *(verb)*
The professor will **invent** a new machine.
create
design
devise

machine *(noun)*
The **machine** made a whirring sound.
appliance
gadget
contraption

mix *(verb)*
You must **mix** the two chemicals together.
blend
combine

poisonous *(adjective)*
The gas is **poisonous**.
deadly
harmful
toxic

prove *(verb)*
Can you **prove** which material is strongest?
confirm
demonstrate
show

runny *(adjective)*
The mixture is **runny**.
liquid
molten
sloppy

sure *(adjective)*
I'm **sure** it'll work.
certain
confident
convinced
hopeful

think about *(verb)*
They had to **think about** the experiment's results.
consider
contemplate
ponder

tool *(noun)*
Which **tool** do you want?
implement
instrument
utensil

Robots

loud *(adjective)*
The <u>loud</u> robot could be heard from far away.
noisy
booming

shake *(verb)*
The robot started to <u>shake</u> as it came to life.
rattle
shudder
vibrate

switch *(noun)*
Use the <u>switch</u> to turn the robot on.
button
control
knob

turn *(verb)*
Four cogs <u>turn</u> inside the robot's head.
go around
rotate

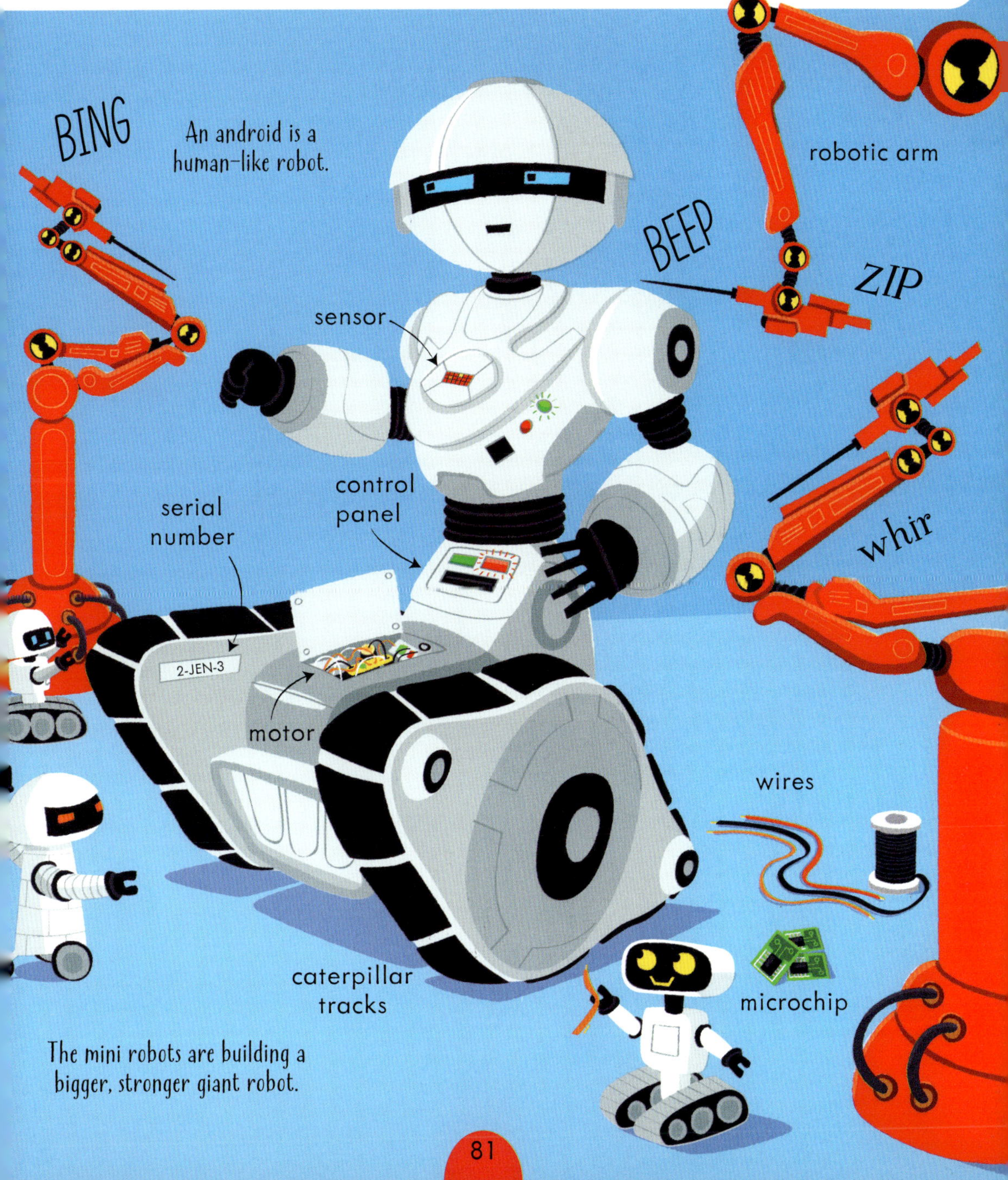

Spooky words

spooky *(adjective)*
This place is too <u>spooky</u> for me.

creepy
eerie
frightening
scary
terrifying

Spooky places

creak *(verb)*
The hinges <u>creak</u> as I open the door.

groan
squeak

dim *(adjective)*
The graveyard was dark and <u>dim</u>.

dingy
gloomy
shadowy

old *(adjective)*
The <u>old</u> house stood alone on a hill.

ancient
crumbling
dilapidated

strange *(adjective)*
A <u>strange</u> noise came from inside the coffin.

mysterious
odd
peculiar
unusual

Writing about spooky things

awful *(adjective)*
He'd never seen such an **awful** sight.

dreadful
gruesome
horrible
revolting
errible

evil *(adjective)*
he **evil** witch sneered.

cruel
vile
wicked

ghost *(noun)*
The **ghost** flew out from the shadows.

ghoul
phantom
spirit

scare *(verb)*
"You can't **scare** me," yelled Amelia.

frighten
petrify
spook
startle
terrify

scream *(verb)*
Someone suddenly started to **scream**.

howl
shriek
screech
wail

shake *(verb)*
She began to **shake** with fear.

tremble
shudder
quake

Vampires...
have fangs
suck blood
wear capes

Witches...
cackle
cast spells
have warty skin
ride broomsticks

Ghosts...
float
haunt
vanish

Fairytale words

adventure *(noun)*
The hero described his last **adventure**.
exploit
feat
quest

anger *(noun)*
The giant bared his teeth in **anger**.
fury
indignation
rage
wrath

astonish *(verb)*
The riches inside the palace will **astonish** you.
amaze
astound
dazzle
stun

beware of *(verb)*
Beware of the three-headed dog.
look out for
steer clear of
watch out for

charm *(verb)*
The fairy queen cast a spell to **charm** the goblins.
beguile
bewitch
enchant
mesmerize

grand *(adjective)*
We spied a **grand** castle through the trees.
fabulous
impressive
magnificent
splendid

hold *(verb)*
She was too afraid to **hold** her wand.
clasp
clutch
grasp
grip

imaginary *(adjective)*
All kinds of **imaginary** creatures live here.
fantastic
make-believe
fictional
mythical

magic *(noun)*
The wizard had studied **magic** all his life.
sorcery
witchcraft
wizardry

real *(adjective)*
The events in this story are not all **real**.
factual
genuine
true
truthful

spell *(noun)*
She muttered a **spell** under her breath.
charm
curse
magic formula

vanish *(verb)*
How did the pixie **vanish**?
disappear
vanish into thin air
become invisible

Fairytale places

castle
cave
dell
dungeon
magical forest
maze
palace
secret passage
tower
treasure room
tunnel
under the sea

Characters and creatures

witch *(noun)*
The wicked **witch** cast an evil spell.

crone
sorceress

wizard *(noun)*
The **wizard** stroked his beard.

magician
sorcerer

Other characters:
dragon
dwarf
elf
giant
goblin
king
knight
magician
mermaid
ogre
prince
princess
queen
troll
unicorn

Fairytale characters can be...
bewitching
creepy
cunning
evil
invisible
kindly
legendary
magical
menacing
under a spell
wicked
wise

Fairytale characters can...
come to the rescue
do battle
have dreams
outwit each other
rescue captives
solve riddles
grant wishes
turn people into stone

Magical things

cloak
crystal ball
lucky charm
magic potions
magic ring
pointed hat
spell book
staff
wand

The dragon slept on the gleaming treasure with one eye always open.

Dinosaurs

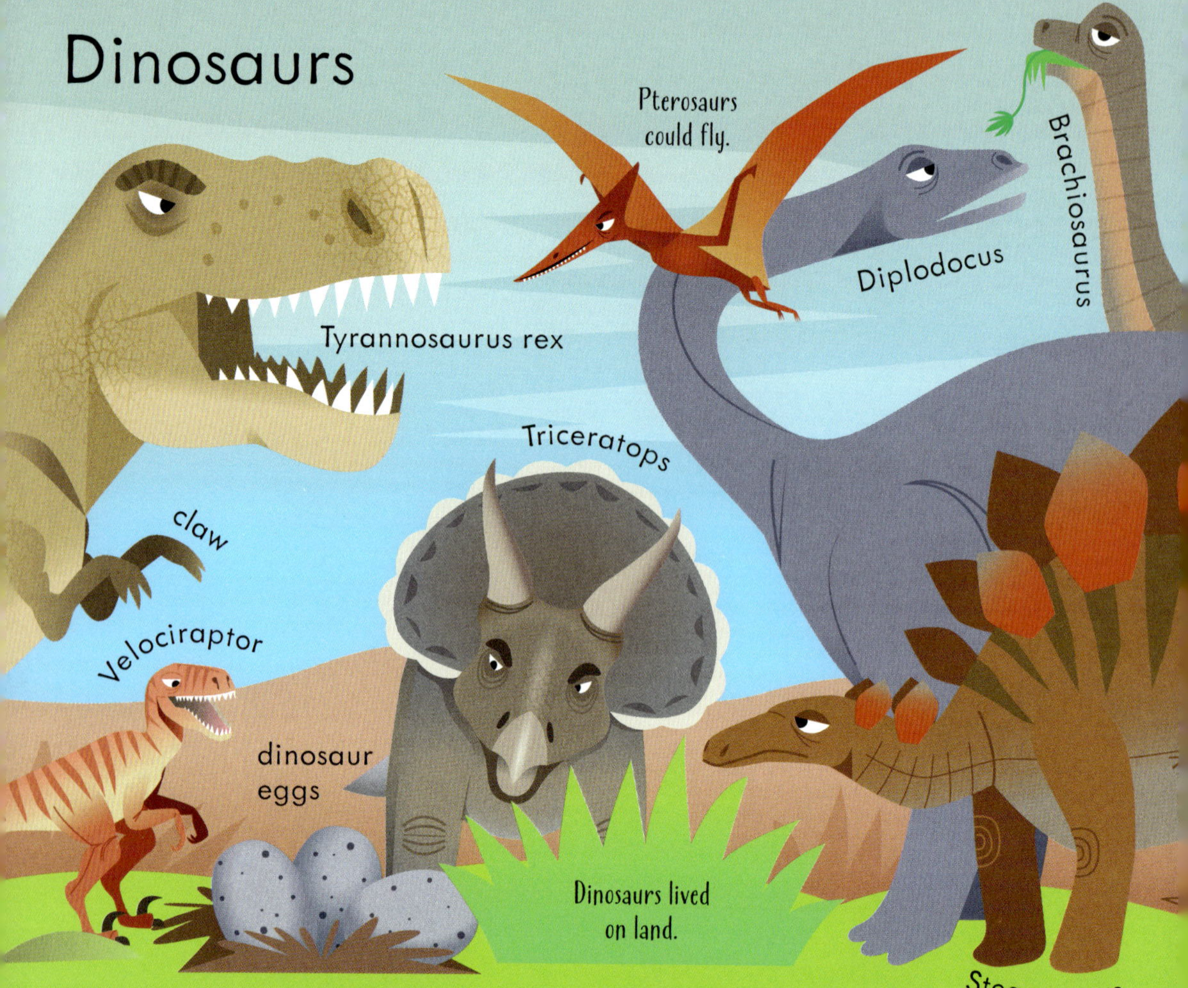

Pterosaurs could fly.

Brachiosaurus

Diplodocus

Tyrannosaurus rex

Triceratops

claw

Velociraptor

dinosaur eggs

Dinosaurs lived on land.

Stegosaurus

Describing dinosaurs

fierce *(adjective)*
A **fierce** Tyrannosaurus loomed above.

aggressive
ferocious
savage
vicious

huge *(adjective)*
Brachiosaurus had a **huge** body.

colossal
enormous
gigantic
massive

strong *(adjective)*
The dinosaur snapped with its **strong** jaws.

mighty
powerful

Dinosaurs can also be...
feathery
meat-eating
scaly

Things dinosaurs do

attack *(verb)*
Velociraptors **attack** each other.

charge at
set upon

land on *(verb)*
The pterosaurs **land on** high branches.

fly down onto
settle on

scratch *(verb)*
They **scratch** the dust with their claws.

gouge
mark
scrape

stare *(verb)*
They **stare** at their prey.

gape
gaze

Jurassic squid

Plesiosaurs lived in the sea.

Cavemen

cave *(noun)*
cavern
Inside the cave it's safe and warm, while outside wild animals roam.
stalactite
volcano
cave painting
woolly mammoth
explode *(verb)*
Lava began to explode from the crater.
erupt
spew
saber-toothed tiger
pick *(verb)*
Some cavemen pick wild berries.
collect
forage
gather
pluck
wild *(adjective)*
They hide from a wild cat.
feral
untamed
stop *(verb)*
They stop hunting and go back home.
finish
give up
quit
stalagmite
burn *(verb)*
The logs in the fire burn bright.
blaze
glow
smolder
animal skin
shelter *(noun)*
They find shelter in the cave.
cover
protection
refuge
spear

Ancient Egypt

age *(noun)*
The pyramid was built in the Ancient Egyptian **age**.
era
period
time

discover *(verb)*
When did they **discover** the tomb?
find
locate
uncover
unearth

fragile *(adjective)*
The jar was made from **fragile** clay.
breakable
brittle
delicate

important *(adjective)*
An **important** nobleman was buried here.
distinguished
notable
remarkable
significant
special

rich *(adjective)*
Rich Egyptians had lots of servants.
affluent
wealthy
well-off

tunnel *(noun)*
A long **tunnel** led to the chamber.
passage
passageway
shaft

Vikings

Describing Vikings

Vikings can be...
ax-wielding
barbaric
brutal
fearsome
ruthless

argue *(verb)*
"Don't **argue**!" ordered the chief.
bicker
quarrel
fight
squabble

crowd *(noun)*
A **crowd** of Vikings set sail.
gang
group
horde
throng

danger *(noun)*
They overcame one **danger** after another.
hazard
peril
threat
trouble

free *(verb)*
Free the captives!
liberate
release
set free

invade *(verb)*
They're about to **invade** the town.
attack
overrun
plunder
raid
storm
take over

store *(noun)*
They ransacked the town's **store** of grain.
hoard
stock
supply

Viking names

Female names:
Astrid
Dagrun
Gudrun
Hilde
Saga
Sigrid

Male names:
Gunnar
Harald
Knut
Leif
Olav
Ulf

Wild West

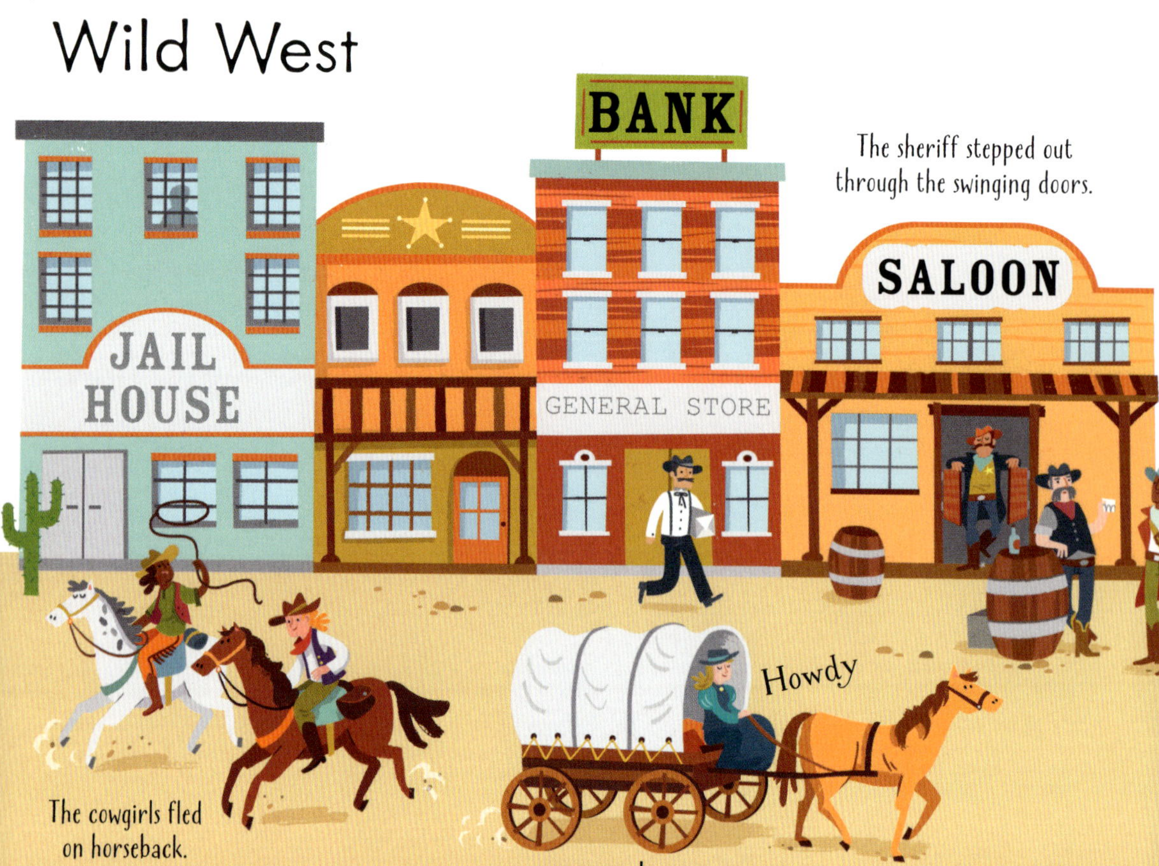

arrest *(verb)*
The sheriff and his deputy plotted to **arrest** the gang.
catch
capture
apprehend

cunning *(adjective)*
The **cunning** cowboy sneaked by unnoticed.
crafty
devious
sly
sneaky
wily

escape *(verb)*
How did they **escape**?
break free
flee
get away
run away

fight *(noun)*
Everyone stopped to watch the **fight**.
brawl
scuffle
tussle

gang *(noun)*
A **gang** of cowgirls rode into town.
group
mob
posse

jail *(noun)*
The man went to **jail** for rustling cattle.
a lock up
prison

luck *(noun)*
The cowboy hit the target by **luck**.
accident
chance
coincidence
fluke

meeting *(noun)*
The deputy summoned everyone to a **meeting**.
assembly
gathering

robber *(noun)*
The **robber** was behind bars at last.
thief
burglar
criminal
crook
bandit

shock *(noun)*
It was a **shock** when he won the rodeo.
surprise
bombshell

steal *(verb)*
The thief tried to **steal** the gold.
grab
snatch
seize
make off with

surprise *(verb)*
Did her horse's speed **surprise** you?
shock
stun
startle

Cowboy words

bronco (wild horse)
cactus
corral (animal pen)
horseshoe
rattlesnake
rodeo (cowboy skills competition)

Characters

cattle rustler (someone who steals cows)
cowboys
cowgirls
sheriff
deputy
townspeople

Story endings

Clutching his wounded arm, the lone cowboy stumbled into the sunset.

The outlaws mounted their horses and rode away in a cloud of dust.

The town of Little Cactus would never be the same again.

Ancient Greeks

temple

old *(adjective)*
The temple is old.
ancient
antiquated

agora
(market place)

A slave broke his shackles and fled from his master.

ruins

choose *(verb)*
The citizens voted to choose their leader.
pick
elect
appoint
select

plan *(verb)*
What did they plan to do?
intend
mean
resolve

message *(noun)*
A boy arrived with a message.
announcement
letter
note
report

Ancient Greek religion

god *(noun)*
The Ancient Greeks believed in more than one god.
deity
divinity

religion *(noun)*
Their religion has lots of stories.
belief
faith

Zeus (king of the gods)

Some Greek gods:
Aphrodite (goddess of love)
Apollo (god of music)
Ares (god of war)
Athena (goddess of wisdom)
Hades (god of the underworld)
Hera (queen of the gods)
Poseidon (god of the sea)

Artemis (goddess of hunting)

Hermes (messenger of the gods)

Romans

denarius (a silver coin)

A Roman man wore a long length of cloth, or toga.

laurel wreath

emperor (ruler of Roman empire)

toga

scroll

senator (politician)

A Roman woman wore a long dress called a stola.

gladius (a sword)

shield

trident (three-pronged spear)

net

Gladiators fought in an arena at an amphitheater.

spear

chariot

Roman names

Augusta
Claudius
Commodus
Faustina
Flavia
Lesbia
Marcus
Octavius
Pompeia
Publius

Male names end in –us and female names in –a.

fight *(verb)*
They watched the gladiators **fight**.
brawl
scuffle
tussle
wrestle

forgive *(verb)*
Will the emperor **forgive** the gladiator if he loses?
excuse
let off
pardon

powerful *(adjective)*
He was a **powerful** ruler.
commanding
forceful
mighty

rebel *(verb)*
The emperor feared the people would **rebel**.
revolt
riot
rise up

In space

astronaut *(noun)*
The <u>astronaut</u> put on his helmet.
space traveler
cosmonaut

explore *(verb)*
Their mission was to <u>explore</u> outer space.
search
tour

orbit *(verb)*
Moons <u>orbit</u> planets.
go around
travel around

shine *(verb)*
Stars <u>shine</u> brightly in the sky.
gleam
glimmer
glow
sparkle
twinkle

spaceship *(noun)*
The <u>spaceship</u> landed on the moon.
rocket
spacecraft

Spaceships may...
take off
blast off
touch down
zoom

Planets can be...
airless
fiery
frozen
icy
rocky

Aliens

alien *(noun)*
martian
space creature
extraterrestrial
lifeform

Describing aliens

evil *(adjective)*
The evil aliens plotted revenge.
nasty
fiendish
wicked

friendly *(adjective)*
The friendly alien came in peace.
gentle
good-natured
kind

Aliens can also be...
green-skinned
one-eyed
slimy
spotted
superintelligent

Things aliens and flying saucers do

attack *(verb)*
Hostile creatures attack the planet.
invade
bombard
storm

bang *(noun)*
His spacecraft landed with a bang.
crash
thud
thump

flash *(verb)*
Flames flash from the engine.
blaze
burst
flare

shoot *(verb)*
Some flying saucers shoot lasers.
aim
direct
fire

Pirates

Pirates are...

adventurous
barbaric
bloodthirsty
bold
brutal
daring
dastardly
lawless
ruthless
swashbuckling
villainous

Pirates...
board ships
bury treasure
drop anchor
make prisoners
walk the plank
plunder
raid
swab (clean) the deck
take prisoners

Pirate ships

crew *(noun)*
The **crew** set sail for home.

sailors
seafarers
mariners

flap *(verb)*
Sails **flap** in the wind.

flutter
ripple
swish

sail *(verb)*
The ship began to **sail**.

cruise
glide
ride the waves

sink *(verb)*
I fear the ship will **sink**.

capsize
go under
founder
submerge

Sea words

crash *(verb)*
Can you hear the waves **crash**?

roar
rumble
thunder

sea *(noun)*
They sailed across the **sea**.

high seas
deep
ocean
waves

sharp *(adjective)*
Sharp rocks ahead!

craggy
jagged

splash *(verb)*
The waves **splash** on the shore.

slap
spill

wave *(noun)*
The bottle was carried by the **wave**.

breaker
surf
swell

wavy *(adjective)*
The sea is **wavy** today.

choppy
fierce
rough
wild

Treasure words

chest *(noun)*
The treasure **chest** was full to the brim.

case
casket
coffer
trunk

shiny *(adjective)*
The **shiny** treasure glinted in the sun.

dazzling
gleaming
glittering
shining
polished
shimmering
sparkling

treasure *(noun)*
Captain Patch dreamed of **treasure**.

bounty
loot
riches

Items of treasure:
coins
ducats
doubloons
goblets
gold
jewels
medallions
pieces of eight
silver

Story starters

"Gold beyond your wildest dreams!" promised the captain...

The treasure map was theirs at last...

Two ships were racing toward Porpoise Island...

YOHOHO
Aaaarr matey
sail
first mate
Jolly Roger
crow's nest
mast
Shiver me timbers
captain
cabin boy
figurehead
BANG
BOOM
BLAST
cannon
portholes
SCREECH
bottlenose dolphin
message in a bottle
cutlass
eyepatch
palm tree
treasure map
hermit crab
breeches
starfish
conch shell
pegleg

Heroes and villains

MEET THE HEROES...

power *(noun)*
Each hero has a different <u>**power**</u>.

ability
force
strength

incredible *(adjective)*
Jet could fly at <u>**incredible**</u> speeds.

amazing
astonishing
astounding
awesome
extraordinary
fantastic
impressive
spectacular
wonderful

nimble *(adjective)*
Basilisk is <u>**nimble**</u> on his feet.

acrobatic
agile
light-footed

climb *(verb)*
Hedera can <u>**climb**</u> a skyscraper in the blink of an eye.

ascend

strong *(adjective)*
Cronos is so <u>**strong**</u> he can lift a car.

brawny
mighty
muscly
muscular
powerful
strapping
tough

amaze *(verb)*
Their powers <u>**amaze**</u> everyone.

astonish
astound
impress
surprise

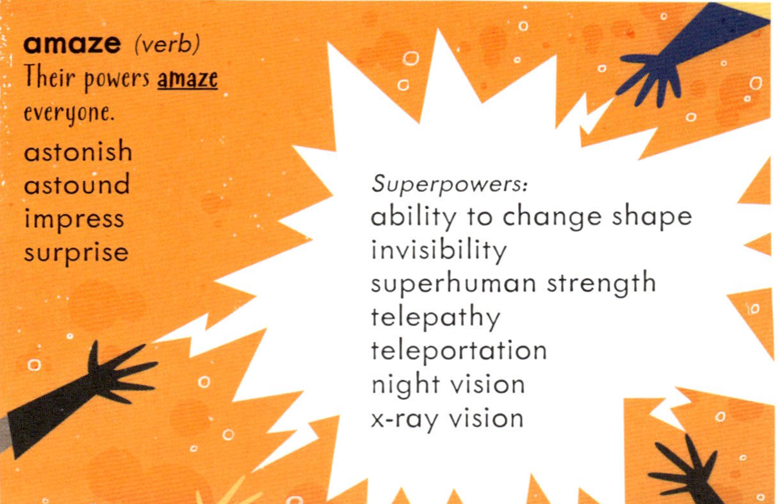

Superpowers:
ability to change shape
invisibility
superhuman strength
telepathy
teleportation
night vision
x-ray vision

MEANWHILE...

villain *(adjective)*
A villain plots in his lair.

bad guy
criminal
mastermind
crook
mischief-maker
scoundrel

proud *(adjective)*
He's as proud as he's cunning.

arrogant
haughty
pompous
smug
vain

boast *(verb)*
He dares to boast about his plan.

brag
gloat

disaster *(noun)*
Disaster threatens the city.

calamity
catastrophe
tragedy

help *(verb)*
"Who will help us?" the people cry out.

aid
assist
support

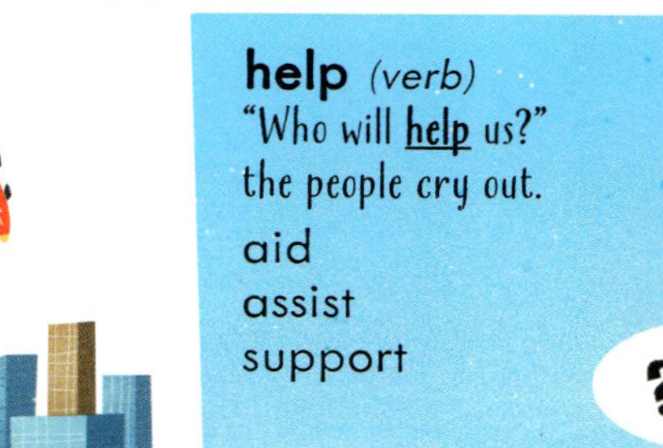

defend *(verb)*
"We will defend you!"

protect
shield

punch *(verb)*
Together they punch the missile and knock it off course.

hit
jab
smack
strike
thump
thwack

stop *(verb)*
The heroes stop the villain's plans.

end
foil
put a stop to

THE END

save *(verb)*
When will the heroes have to save the city again?

rescue

Knights and castles

Describing knights

alert *(adjective)*
Sir Gawain was ready and alert.
attentive
watchful
wide-awake

brave *(adjective)*
There was no knight more brave.
bold
courageous
daring
gallant
heroic
plucky

cruel *(adjective)*
The cruel knight vowed revenge on the whole town.
callous
merciless
pitiless
ruthless

Knights can also be...
chivalrous
fearless
honorable
lionhearted
noble
quick-witted

Armor and weapons

flail
mace
plume
helmet
breastplate
chainmail
shield
gauntlet
greave
spur
dagger
broadsword

Things knights do

courage *(noun)*
Knights show great courage.
bravery
fearlessness
valor

fight *(verb)*
Armies of knights will fight.
clash
cross swords
do battle
take up arms
wage war

guard *(verb)*
He was told to guard the gate.
defend
protect
watch

mission *(noun)*
The knights were training for their next mission.
adventure
expedition
quest

stab *(verb)*
A knight can stab his sword.
jab
lunge with
thrust

swear *(verb)*
Will you swear to protect the king?
promise
vow

In battle

enemy *(noun)*
The army fought the enemy for days.
opponent
opposition
other side

retreat *(verb)*
The soldiers began to retreat.
flee
move back
withdraw

At a joust

admire *(verb)*
The crowds admire the dashing knight.
look up to
marvel at
respect

cheer *(verb)*
They will cheer if he wins.
applaud
clap
whoop

castle *(noun)*
chateau
fort
fortress
keep
palace
stronghold

battle *(noun)*
clash
conflict
skirmish

Monsters

monster *(noun)*
beast
creature

Monsters can be...
bloodthirsty
deadly
fire-breathing
gigantic
hairy
long-necked
one-eyed
scaly
slimy
tough
wrinkly

Monsters can have...
claws
fangs
fur
hairy toes
horns
rotten breath
scales
spines
tails
warts
wings

A monster might live in a...
bog
castle
cave
dell
den
dungeon
forest
lair
lake
swamp
well

brutal *(adjective)*
Everyone feared the **brutal** creature.
brutish
fearsome
ferocious
fierce
savage

smell *(noun)*
A **smell** wafted from the ogre's boots.
odor
stench

stink *(verb)*
The goblin's clothes **stink**.
smell
reek

tangled *(adjective)*
Its fur was greasy and **tangled**.
knotted
matted
twisted

tough *(adjective)*
That giant is a **tough** brute.
wild
rough
violent
vicious
hard

unpleasant *(adjective)*
The **unpleasant** troll lived by himself.
nasty
disagreeable
bad-tempered
spiteful

Things monsters do

annoy *(verb)*
The gremlins **annoy** the villagers.
pester
harass
harangue
trouble

lie *(verb)*
The deceitful goblin couldn't help but **lie**.
fib
tell lies
tell untruths

shock *(verb)*
Did its groans **shock** you too?
alarm
scare
startle
surprise

smear *(verb)*
The swamp monsters **smear** the walls with gunk.
daub
rub
spread

squash *(verb)*
The giant tried to **squash** the house with her foot.
crumple
crush
flatten
smash
squish
stomp on
trample on

temper *(noun)*
The grumpy monster is in a bad **temper**.
mood
rage

Monsters can...
attack without warning
bellow
chomp on food
roar
scratch
slobber
snort
swish their tails

Writing tips

Write your own words

- You can join some words together to make new words.
- Add *-sounding*, *-looking*, *-smelling* or *-tasting* to the end of an adjective, to describe how something sounds, looks, smells or tastes.
- Add *-eating*, *-hating*, *-loving* or *-fearing* after a noun, to describe what something eats, hates, loves or fears.

shrill-sounding birds
a scrawny-looking cat
foul-smelling fruit
delicious-tasting donuts

a cheese-eating mouse
a mailman-hating dog
slime-loving monsters
a clown-fearing ringmaster

POP

Sounds like

- Each of these words is an onomatopeia (*say on-oh-mat-oh-pee-a*).
- An onomatopeia when spoken sounds like the noise it describes.
- Spell out noises to make your own onomatopeia words.

Descriptive comparisons

- You can describe something by comparing it with something else. This is known as a simile.
  - Many similes start with *like*:

Flames burst from the dragon's mouth like molten lava from an erupting volcano.

- Similes can also start with *as*:

The wet ground was as slippery as an ice rink.

Setting the scene

- Describe scenes as fully as you can when writing stories.

  Describe...
  - what the weather is like
  - what noises can be heard
  - how the surroundings look, smell, feel or taste

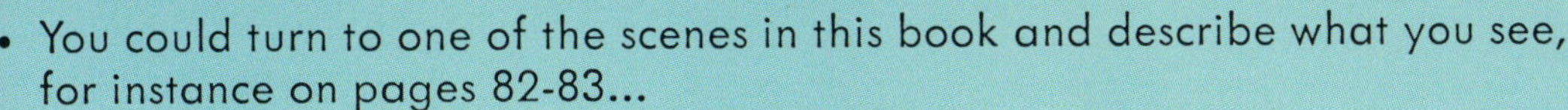

- You could turn to one of the scenes in this book and describe what you see, for instance on pages 82-83...

A bolt of lightning lit up the night sky revealing a lonely house on a hill. In the distance a wolf howled while bats squeaked overhead. The air around them was damp, and thick with the smell of rotten eggs...

Characters

- Describe your characters thoroughly to make them convincing.

  Write about...
  - what they look like
  - how they move
  - how they talk
  - their personalities

"My name is Oz," bellowed the burly caveman. Wiry hairs sprouted from his ears and yellow teeth crowded his mouth. His clothes were tattered and frayed, and he waddled as he walked...

Dramatic writing

To make your writing exciting...
- keep your sentences short and punchy
- use lots of different verbs
- avoid using too many adverbs

The hungry chameleon had spotted its prey. It inched along the leaf. It aimed its mouth. With a flash of pink, its tongue shot out...

Conversation

- Try not to use the word *said* every time you write what someone says.
- Look for alternatives on page 32.
- Think about the way your character is talking, to help you to choose the right word.

"I'm sorry," whimpered Ant.

"I've never been so happy," bragged Henry.

Word games

These games are for two or more people to play.

A–Z game

- Choose a category such as food.
- Everyone then has to say a type of food that begins with each letter of the alphabet, starting with *A*.
- You could make the game trickier by deciding that everyone must describe their word with an adjective beginning with the same letter.

Other categories:

Animals
Hobbies
Names
Places

Story chain

- Take turns saying one word at a time to make up a story.
- See how far you can go until someone can't think of a word.

Tip: words such as *but* and *however* will help you to continue the story.

Word duel

- Pick a word from the list on the right.
- You have two minutes to think of, and maybe write down, as many words with a similar meaning as you can.
- Then take turns saying one word at a time until someone runs out of ideas.

Words:

hot
cold
happy
sad
good
bad
tasty
beautiful
big
small
eat
scary
nice
run
said

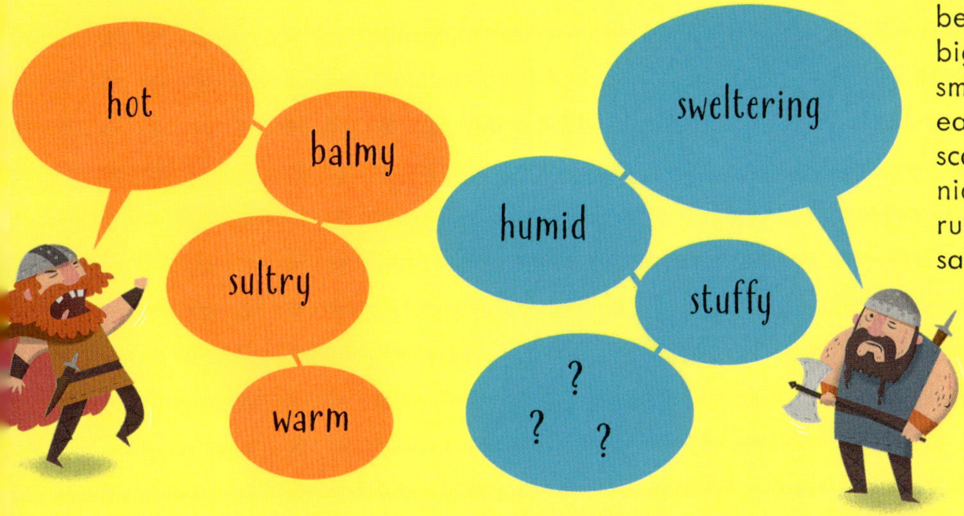
hot
balmy
sultry
warm
sweltering
humid
stuffy
?
? ?

Word association

- Whoever goes first says a word.
- The next person has to say another word linked to that word.
- Each player has to keep saying a word associated with the word before it.

For example:

boat... beach... sand... castle... knight... horse...

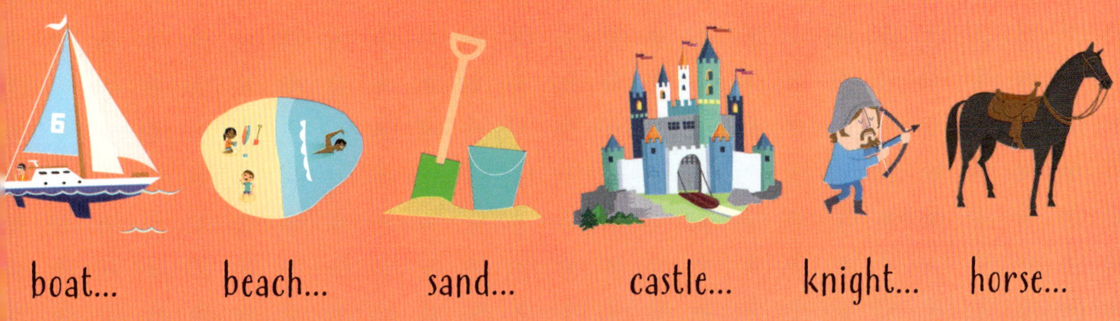

Word finder

If you want to find alternatives to a particular word, you can look it up in this word finder. It will tell you where there are other words to use instead.

a

b

A B C D E F G H I J K L M N O P Q R S T U V W X Y Z

C

A B C D E F G H I J K L M N O P Q R S T U V W X Y Z

A B C D E F G H I J K L M N O P Q R S T U V W X Y Z

d

e

A
B
C
D
E
F
G
H
I
J
K
L
M
N
O
P
Q
R
S
T
U
V
W
X
Y
Z

f

g

A B C D E F G H I J K L M N O P Q R S T U V W X Y Z

h

i

j

A B C D E F G H I J K L M N O P Q R S T U V W X Y Z

k

l

m

A B C D E F G H I J K L M N O P Q R S T U V W X Y Z

n

o

p

q

r

s

A B C D E F G H I J K L M N O P Q R S T U V W X Y Z

t

U

V

W

X Y Z

Usborne Quicklinks

To visit websites where you can find more writing tips and word games to play, go to the Usborne Quicklinks website at www.usborne.com/quicklinks and type in the keyword 'thesaurus'.

When using the internet please follow the internet safety guidelines displayed at the Usborne Quicklinks website. The recommended websites are regularly reviewed and the links at Usborne Quicklinks are updated. However, Usborne Publishing is not responsible and does not accept liability for the content or availability of any website other than its own. We recommend that children are supervised while on the internet.

First published in 2015 by Usborne Publishing Ltd., 83-85 Saffron Hill, London EC1N 8RT, England. www.usborne.com

First published in America 2015. AE.